ABOUT THE AUTHOR

Glen Humphries is a multi award-winning journalist and author. He was named the beer writer of the year at the Australian International Beer Awards. His first book, *The Slab*, was the national winner in the worldwide Gourmand Food and Drink Writing awards. He has written six other books, all published via his own Last Day of School publishing imprint.

I0085477

Also by Glen Humphries and published by Last Day of School
(www.lastdayofschool.net)

The Slab: 24 Stories of Beer in Australia

James Squire: The Biography

The Six-Pack: Stories from the World of Beer

Friday Night at the Oxford

Beer Is Fun

Sounds Like an Ending: Midnight Oil, 10-1 and Red Sails in the Sunset

Night Terrors
The true story of the Kingsgrove Slasher

Glen Humphries

Last Day of School
www.lastdayofschool.net

ISBN: 978-0-6480323-7-3

A catalogue record of this book is available from the National Library of Australia.

This book is dedicated to Margaret, Marlene, Lesley, Anne, Gloria, Annette, Valerie, Rosalie, Georgina, Lorraine, Robin, Marguerite, Elaine, Dale Helen D, Mona and Helen G.

1

"Who is the Kingsgrove Slasher? Identify him and run him to earth at all costs!"
Police Commissioner Delaney, *The Sun*, December 21, 1956

They called them slasher bars. Steel or iron bars over windows, attached to the brickwork of houses in a number of suburbs west of the city of Sydney. Suburbs like Kingsgrove, Earlwood, Bardwell Park and Beverly Hills. If you drive through these suburbs today you can still see the bars here and there on the older houses, those that would have been standing in the 1950s.

Normally bars are used to keep someone inside from getting out, but in the late 1950s it was the other way around; those bars were installed by worried residents keen to stop someone outside from getting in. That person became known as the Kingsgrove Slasher, a terrifying figure who would climb into women's bedrooms armed with a razor and slash them while they slept.

He would eventually be caught and plead guilty to 18 crimes, though it's highly likely there were others. He was a man quite sure he was smarter than the police and showed no inclination to volunteer any crimes the cops hadn't already decided were his handiwork.

Today the M5 Motorway cuts straight through the heart of what was the Slasher's territory from 1956-59. That road taking people into Sydney at 80km/h runs through tunnels under some of the homes the Slasher entered, cuts in two streets where victims lived and, in one case, saw the demolition of a home where he assaulted a teenage girl while she slept in her own bed.

For many, the Slasher's crimes are forgotten despite the presence of those slasher bars in suburbia. There are some who know of him but who believe his crimes to be minor and subject to exaggeration with the passage of time. In his autobiography comedian Grahame Bond – who lived not far from Slasher territory in the 1950s – misleadingly described him as a man who "would merrily slash through ladies' flyscreens and breathe heavily at their bedsides while he watched them sleep." Actress Jacki Weaver, who also grew up in Slasher territory, had a more realistic view; for her he was "a serial prowler who broke into women's bedrooms and slashed them with a razor blade while they were sleeping".

Suburban Sydney in the late 1950s was genuinely afraid of the Kingsgrove Slasher. Those who couldn't afford slasher bars put nails in their window frames so they couldn't be opened (even in the heat of a Sydney summer), women slept with hammers and sharp knives beside their bed, vigilantes walked the streets, residents started up neighbourhood patrols and any man spotted out late at night would be stopped and quizzed by police.

The Sun, *The Mirror* and *The Telegraph* all gave over their front pages to his crimes – as well as those of apparent copycats. Those afternoon tabloids covered the committal hearing in great detail; it was front page news and splashed across several pages inside for three or four days. The trial itself got a similar degree of newspaper acreage. The concern about the Slasher and his crimes was so great it even managed to force the *Sydney Morning Herald*, which was a more staid, conservative paper than it is now, to devote space to following the story.

There is the perception that the 1950s were a more innocent time, an era devoid of serious crime compared to today. Yes, there are some strong differences between then and now. In the 1950s, shops closed on Sundays, you couldn't get a drink in a pub after 6pm, people pumped your petrol at service stations, marijuana was unheard of, smoking wasn't considered a health hazard and *Playboy* magazine was still banned.

But the criminals of the 1950s could still be violent and cruel. The residents who slept clutching hammers, who walked the streets at night accosting anyone who looked suspicious had a right to be concerned. The Slasher was far more than some harmless pervert who liked to watch women sleep. He punched a 21-year-old woman in the mouth so hard he broke her teeth and knocked her unconscious. She nearly choked to death on her own blood. Another victim, aged 64, was slashed so deeply across the abdomen she almost died from loss of blood. An 18-year-old girl was hit across the face with a lump of wood while several others – one as young as 13 – woke up while being groped and fondled by a stranger in their bedroom. He even slashed the bedding of a sleeping seven-year-old girl.

If these crimes occurred today they would stoke the same feelings of outrage and fear as they did in the late 1950s. And yet today, the Slasher's rampage is all but forgotten, perhaps in part because no one was killed or raped. Or perhaps because so few people know the truth of what he did. Even today there has been precious little written about those years of fear between 1956 and 1959, and much of what has been written is incorrect.

The bulk of this book is drawn on the detailed contemporary newspaper coverage of the Kingsgrove Slasher case, which regularly made the front pages of the afternoon tabloids, and the court transcripts from the Slasher's committal hearing and trial. At the conclusion of the 1959 committal the magistrate sealed all the court documents for 75 years. After appealing to the court, I was able to access the court transcript, likely the first time anyone had cast eyes on them since 1959.

Any dialogue that appears in quotes comes from either a newspaper interview with the person or the court transcripts. If it appears in quotes it's because the person said it – there is no invented dialogue in *Night Terrors*. Similarly all descriptions of the crime scenes and what the Slasher did come from newspaper coverage or the Slasher's own words from the police questioning.

My interest in the Slasher is because I grew up in Kingsgrove in the 1970s and heard tales from my cousin about the Slasher's exploits. To add a level of tension to my childhood imaginings, the house we lived in was the same one my father and his two sisters grew up in back in the 1950s when the Slasher was on the prowl.

Located in what was a well-developed section of Kingsgrove with no vacant land or nearby bush, it meant my dad and his sisters were safe from a visit. The Slasher's preference was to enter houses close to reserves, scrubland or railway lines so as to give himself a camouflaged escape route. That was only known with the benefit of hindsight; at the time he was on the streets there was no reason to think the man with the razor wouldn't climb through my aunt's bedroom window.

My dad can still remember the terror that gripped the area at the time. Doors and windows at home were locked and any man outside after dark was likely to be stopped and questioned by police. He suggested there was a rumour going around at the time that, unbeknownst to the police, they stopped the Slasher himself for questioning one night. Accepting his story that he was out on a training run, they let him go. While the Slasher's public face was a convincing one – even after he was caught, some could not believe such a nice man could be responsible for these horrible crimes – and his charm probably could have allayed police superstitions during a night-time stop, I could find not even the slightest evidence of this actually happening. Perhaps the answer lies deep in some dusty case files in a police records storage area.

My dad also remembers regularly hearing the sirens of police cars at all hours of the night; either responding to a Slasher call or just flying the colours to show the locals the police were on the case. Given the prevalence of faked Slasher attacks, it's likely to be the former. According to my father, there was also the belief that the truth of the Slasher's attacks was kept from the public; that he actually raped a number of his victims. There is no evidence of this and, in fact the lead detective on the Slasher Patrol – Detective Sergeant Brian Doyle – would testify in court that nothing of the sort happened. The detective had a strong reputation as an honest copper, so it's unlikely he would have lied on the stand.

So *Night Terrors* was inspired by the idea to find out what really happened; to sort out the truth from the family stories. It turned out those family stories had been exaggerated but, as you're about to find out, there was no need. The real story about those years of suburban terror was frightening enough on its own.

2

"Doctor, sister killed in car bomb outrage at Kingsgrove"
Sydney Morning Herald, August, 14, 1956

Even without a dark shape walking through suburban streets at night carrying a razor in his pocket and deviousness on his mind, it's likely Kingsgrove would have achieved a degree of notoriety in 1956. That was due to the combination of a gas explosion and a bizarre case involving a car bomb, suicide and a desire for one of the participants to donate their eyes to science.

At 6am on February 15, a loud boom echoed across Kingsgrove. Residents rushed to their windows, flicked aside the curtains and looked out to see a large mushroom cloud forming over the suburb. The source was the Australian Gas Light Company-owned gasometer – a large metal tank for storing gas – along the downward slope of Kingsgrove Road from its intersection with Homer Street. The top of the tank had ruptured, causing the millions of litres of gas inside to leak out and create a sudden loss of pressure in the tank. That saw the structure collapse within the steel framework built to support it, not unlike a crushed aluminium can. As it fell it made an ominous rumbling sound before the friction from the tank scraping alongside the supports caused sparks and ignited the leaking gas. The flash of the ignition was so bright it was reportedly seen 20 kilometres away.

The fire scorched the earth and vegetation for more than 400 metres around the tank and the force of the blast sent tar, molten metal and debris over homes half a kilometre away. Those living in houses nearby had rushed out of their front doors in terror – still wearing pajamas and nightgowns – after the early morning explosion. Five people had to be treated for burns, four of whom were at work at the bus depot a few hundred metres away. Bus driver Harold Kelly was thrown off his feet by the explosion, the hands of his watch were twisted and the leather wristband scorched.

A test pilot with TAA was on a training flight 500 metres above the gasometer and saw a mushroom cloud forming. "The column of smoke shot up in front of us," he said. "It went up at least 300ft [90 metres] higher than we were."

Covering it on page four of the following day's paper, a *Sydney Morning Herald* reporter spoke to the gasometer's next-door neighbour, a Mrs Bentley; the walls in her house were blistered from the heat. "The house shook and the doors rattled. I was terrified. I thought that part of the street had been blown up. I saw people running with their children, running in all directions. It was a frightening sight in the heat and smoke."

Teen Gary Tolra lived in one of the side streets just across the road from the tank. He heard it rumbling in the seconds before the explosion.

"I looked out the window," Tolra said.

"The rumbling was getting louder and I saw the gasometer wobbling about and shaking. Then there was a terrific blast and the flames shot up about 400ft [120 metres]."

In August 1956 came the tragic and bizarre tale that included a double murder, a car bomb, a suicide, claims of medical malpractice, snobbery and an odd donation of body organs.

Around 7pm on Monday, August 13, Dr Edward Brotchie locked up his surgery on Kingsgrove Road in the suburb's CBD just south of the train station. The 50-year-old Brotchie and his 45-year-old sister Elsie Foster – who was working as his receptionist – then crossed the road and headed to Paterson Avenue, where the doctor had parked his pale blue 1955 Plymouth two hours earlier due to parking restrictions on the main drag. Despite living less than 300 metres from his surgery, Dr Brotchie chose to drive to work rather than walk – perhaps to make it easier to go on house calls during the day.

The doctor walked almost to the end of Paterson Ave where he had been able to find a parking space that morning. He unlocked the passenger side to let Foster in and then walked around to the driver's side. Once inside, he slid the key into the ignition, turned it – and the Plymouth exploded.

All four doors of the car were blown open and left dangling loosely on their hinges – but the glass of their windows was unbroken. The hood was blown off and sent almost 50 metres down the street, the roof of the car was peeled back in the blast and metre-high flames roared out. The rear windshield was found intact in a front yard while the rubber waterproofing that had held it in place was hanging from overhead power lines.

Maxwell Schneider and his son Rex had rushed out of their home when they heard the blast. What they saw was a car "opened up like a can of sardines" with flames pouring out. Despite the fire, the father and son ran to the car and soon spotted an arm laying across the front seat in amongst the tangled mess of metal. "I called out to Rex to give me a hand. We both tugged the arm and pulled out the doctor and laid him on the road. He was unconscious but moaned twice."

Foster had been thrown from the vehicle, her legless body was found on the nature strip close to the car. A shoe and her handbag were found in the front yard of a nearby house. Brotchie lost an arm and both legs had been almost completely severed when the bomb detonated. Sister and brother were both just clinging to life; she would die just minutes after arriving at St George Hospital while he passed away 20 minutes after being admitted.

During the explosion and the aftermath, the bomber had sat in his van just 100 metres away. He had driven to Paterson Ave an hour earlier to connect the wires for his bomb, then went home for dinner before returning to see the result of his handiwork. Satisfied, he headed to the hospital to check on the condition of Brotchie and Foster. Then he drove to the doctor's surgery to put the final part of his plan into action.

Back at the scene of the crime, police investigations were continuing. Among the police was Detective Sergeant Brian Doyle a balding, fire-plug of a man with a reputation for being incorruptible and who would in time solve the Kingsgrove Slasher case. The noise and fire of the blast had brought out the rubberneckers in droves; police and firemen had to link arms and walk down the street to clear them away.

The bomb had blown a large hole through the floor below the driver's seat but an explosives expert could not say whether it was taped to the bottom of the floor or laid on the ground. Estimating the bomb to include around two kilograms of gelignite, he felt it was built by someone who knew what they were doing, the *Herald* reported. "The person who connected the explosive to the car must have known a great deal about this sort of thing. It would take several minutes to connect up the explosive properly."

Standing around the destroyed car, the early suspicions of police leaned towards the possibility that a "mentally unbalanced" patient had enacted some sort of revenge on the doctor. But at that moment, the bomber was no longer in his van but sitting in a chair in the doctor's surgery. With a .22 calibre bullet in his head and a short note in his pocket.

At dawn the following morning police entered Brotchie's surgery and found the body of Henry Foster – Elsie Foster's husband of more than two decades. They read the short note he had left them, which read "You will find letters and my will on a table at home". It didn't take police long to get to Henry and Elsie's home in Vivienne Street – it was just 600 metres from the surgery. Once there, they found scores of books on engineering, science and chemistry, as well as explosives and a number of what the *Sydney Morning Herald* described as "weird gadgets".

There was also a stack of letters left on his dining room table, some dated as early as July 17, which indicated Henry Foster had thought about the night's action for at least a month. One letter, addressed to his sister-in-law Ruby Grenfell (whom he made executor of his will), suggested his fuse had been slowly burning for some time and that he was fine with what he planned to do. "I regret to give you this disturbance but do not worry or blame yourself. It was going to happen months ago but postponed when your wedding was announced. We have all got to die sometime, so if it is a little sooner than later, why worry?". Another letter was addressed to a UK research institute asking to be taken off its mailing list. There was also a confession, described by police as "the writing of a madman". In his confession he admitted to the double murder the night before.

"I am responsible for placing a device in Ed Brotchie's car. He is responsible for igniting it," Foster wrote. Suggesting a degree of self-absorption, his wife had to die because he was going to kill himself; "I knew my wife would not desire to live without me. Our love and life together has been so perfect: few others attain such perfection."

When it came to a motive for the doctor's murder, Foster's words read like the justifications of an unbalanced mind, one that is convinced he was endlessly persecuted by others. At one point he wrote that he was motivated by a row with Brotchie after the doctor poached Foster's office secretary. Elsewhere he alleged malpractice after the doctor had mistreated his back injury to the point Foster needed "special pills" to sleep. Another motive crops up later in the letter where Foster's real target wasn't Brotchie but the doctor's wife, Irene. He claimed she "just ignored" him at a family function and, at his and Elsie's wedding anniversary dinner, she had ruined things by letting her daughter behave in a "disgusting way".

The confession also asked police to donate his corneas to a Sydney eye hospital as "they may be of service to some unfortunate individual with more desire for life than me". He finished the letter with a suicidal take on Shakespeare's famous "To be or not to be" quote from *Hamlet*, with a pair of vertical lines striking out the first two words.

Ongoing investigations by police found that Brotchie knew about the bomb being fitted to his car. He had watched as Foster installed it, having been told by the engineer it was a fuel-saving device that would revolutionise motoring. A 15-centimetre aluminium cylinder, it was attached to the gearbox at one end and two spark plugs welded to the other. Foster had filled the cylinder with nitroglycerine and capped it with a screw. The bomb would remain inert until that Monday night when Foster turned up at Paterson Ave to connect the wires from the spark plugs to the ignition. A fireman and a milkman told the coroner they had seen

Foster – tools in hand – under the hood of Brotchie's Plymouth just over an hour before the explosion.

In one final twist, the bomber and his victims had a joint funeral. On Thursday, August 16, three days after the bomb went off, mourners gathered at the Hurstville Methodist Church for the funerals of Edward Brotchie, Elsie Foster and Henry Foster. The Church reverend said it was proof the Brotchies were "genuine forgiving people".

"The members of the family looked on Mr Foster as a very sick man mentally," Rev JR Brand said. "He had a very close association with the family and the children. The family feels his affliction and frustrations led to his planning of this terrible thing."

While bombs and gas explosions were happening in Kingsgrove in 1956, one man chose that year to start climbing into houses and slashing women as they slept.

3

"You were not aware of any person having inflicted these cuts on you, nor did you see any person or hear any person?"
"No, I didn't see or hear anything."
Margaret Campbell, committal hearing testimony, June 17, 1959

I t started one warm Thursday night in March. It was the last in a streak of warm days. Despite being the middle of the week, thousands of people flocked to Sydney's beaches as the summer heat hung around into early spring. The day before, 6000 people turned up to cool down in the waters of Bondi, at least until two sharks were spotted close to the shoreline and the life-savers sounded the alarm.

By the time it was 10am on that Thursday – March 8, 1956 – the temperature had hit 30 degrees in what the papers were calling the steamiest day in three months. Much to the dismay of beachgoers, some relief came around 3pm when a thunderstorm dumped 24 millimetres of rain in two hours and dropped the mercury by 10 degrees.

It was humid and still at 9.30pm, when Margaret Campbell and a "male friend" (as the court testimony delicately put it) drove from her Hurstville home to scrubland near Beverly Hills train station, just a suburb to the north. These days the area around the station is densely developed but in the 1950s there were still quiet, empty spaces where two people could steal away for some private moments.

Though the 20-year-old Campbell and her male suitor didn't know it, they weren't alone. A dark-haired man in his late 20s had come across the couple's secluded location. He'd spent some months before walking the streets, first throwing water bombs and rocks at passersby before deciding to scale people's back fences and look through windows, and then entering their houses late at night and watching the residents sleep. This warm March night, he was about to take another step up – with the help of the razor in his pocket.

Margaret and her "male escort" (another way the court described the unnamed man) were sitting in the front seat of the car. Because of the warm night both front doors had been opened to allow whatever breeze there was to flow over their bodies. It also allowed the man the chance to watch them unobstructed, which he did for a short while before deciding to put the Gillette Blue razor in his pocket to use.

He crept up to the car in darkness – the couple had switched off the interior light so as not to be seen. Reaching in through the open door, he managed to slash Campbell across the chest around 12 times without being seen. He went back to watch the couple's reaction, before leaving the scene amused they hadn't noticed what he'd done.

Surprisingly for a woman who had been slashed a dozen times, Campbell said she hadn't felt the cuts at first (which perhaps speaks of her male friend's abilities to distract her). Soon she felt a stinging sensation across her chest; Campbell looked down and saw her yellow frock had been cut, and the cuts went through her slip, brasserie and into her skin. There was also blood soaking through her clothes.

The male friend rushed Campbell to Hurstville police station, where an officer took her to see a female doctor in the casualty department at St George Hospital. Dr Claire Burke took a look at Campbell's cuts, of which she estimated there were 12 – most on the breasts while one was in the armpit. While most were superficial, two cuts required stitches – Campbell and Dr Burke would later differ as to how many, she would say there were six while the doctor only remembered three stitches.

There was no doubt some salacious aspects of the Campbell attack. She was in a car with a man in a relatively secluded location, she was slashed by an attacker and she was so distracted by what she and the man were doing that she didn't even notice a stranger creeping up on them and cutting her with a blade. It had the ingredients the tabloid press love, and yet it doesn't seem to have made it into any of the three afternoon tabloids serving Sydney at the time.

Also, for several years afterwards, it would not even be publicly linked to the Kingsgrove Slasher. That connection wouldn't be made until after his capture in mid-1959, three years later, when the committal hearing was held. In their coverage over the Slasher's three-year campaign, the tabloids were keen to lump in any attack as his handiwork and even published maps showing the location of his crimes.

None of those maps ever circled a secluded piece of scrubland near Beverly Hills station. The reason for that would become pretty obvious; of the 18 attacks the Slasher would be jailed for this was the only one that didn't take place in a house. For a man keen to make a habit of cutting women across the chest, prowling around at night looking for a parked car with the doors open was always going to be harder than climbing through a window left slightly open by a home owner to catch the cool breeze. Which is exactly what he did in his second attack, opening of a window of the Storz family home in Vanessa Street, Beverly Hills, and climbing inside.

He would take breaks from prowling over his three years – some of them short, some very long. One of these is the gap after he found Margaret Campbell that night in March. Between that and the night he stood in the yard of the Storz house, four months had passed. One can only conclude he had been in other houses over those four months, but without leaving any trace of his presence. After the Slasher's capture he would list a number of streets in Kingsgrove and the surrounding suburbs where he reckoned he'd been inside every single house. Once inside, he would creep into a bedroom and spy on the family members while they slept, or sit in the darkness of the lounge room and watch as someone got up to go to the toilet. All the while those inside had no idea they were sharing their home with an unwelcome visitor.

That changed in the early hours of July 4. At around 3am, the Slasher was outside the Storz house. It was located along the northern side of the train line between Beverly Hills and Kingsgrove stations, with scrublands across the road (which would become a common geographical feature of the Slasher houses). Carrying an empty petrol drum he'd found in the backyard, the Slasher chose a window that was shielded from the street. Standing on the drum, he quietly pushed the window open and climbed through.

Inside the room were two beds, separated by a simple partition. In one bed slept 12-year-old Marlene Storz and on the other side of the partition was her grandmother Emma Wurst. Also in the house were Marlene's parents, her brother Hans and an aunt and uncle.

Night Terrors

The Slasher paid no attention to the elderly woman and walked over to 12-year-old Marlene's bed. He took out his razor and cut into her blanket and bedsheets several times, leaving gashes as long as 15 centimetres. Unlike Campbell, the slashes did not reach Marlene's skin. The girl then woke up and, still in the grip of sleep, saw a dark figure flitting around at the foot of her bed. Thinking it was her brother, she spoke in German "is that you, Hans?". Spooked, the Slasher immediately jumped out the window and escaped.

Her grandmother would soon tell her family and police that she too had come close to the Slasher. While in a sleep stupor, Mrs Wurst felt the Slasher was her late husband coming back from the dead to see her again. She reached out, placed her arms around the Slasher's neck and said to him "darling, now you have come back, never leave me". When Marlene called out there was a man in the room, she woke up. The Slasher would later claim not to remember any of this, while the grandmother would later insist it had all been a dream.

The public would not hear about what went on in the Storz house, not at first. It wouldn't be until the Slasher had committed a further three crimes in July before the city realised who had been in the house that morning.

4

"Yes, I cut her before I punched her."
The Kingsgrove Slasher's police interview, May 1, 1959

The Slasher may have let four months pass between the day in March he stumbled across Margaret Campbell and when he slipped through a window at the Storz home, but he would not wait anywhere near that long before he tried his luck again. Just 10 days would go by before he would strike again in what turned out to be a violent assault on a helpless woman who had the misfortune of choosing to spend a night with friends.

Twenty-one year-old Lesley Jean Coleman (newspaper reports and court transcripts also spell her first name as "Lesby", though I've gone with the more common name) had been to a ball in town on a Friday night and, because she lived north of the city, chose to stay the night with the Howells, family friends in Colwell Street, Kingsgrove. While the later court testimony is unclear, there is the suggestion she may have been more than just friends with Kevin, one of the family's sons. It wasn't the first time Coleman had stayed with the Howells; she knew them quite well. But after the events of July 24 she would never stay there again.

Night Terrors

The Slasher was very fond of the night. With the exception of his first attack, the Slasher's crimes would all be committed after midnight; this suggested he would spend hours prowling the streets of suburbia. It also hinted that the man didn't have anyone at home who would miss him, who would wonder where he was in the early hours of the morning. When he came to the Howell home in Colwell Street it was some time after 3am on a Saturday. He walked along the driveway that was two lines of concrete with a strip of grass in the middle until he reached a door at the side of the house. Putting his hand on the knob, he twisted and found there was no resistance. When May and Walter Howell had gone to bed, they'd locked all the doors and windows, except for the side door which their son and Coleman would use when they came home from the ball. While the pair had closed the door when they arrived home, the son seemingly forgot to lock it.

The Slasher could hardly believe his luck. Before stepping inside, he went further down the backyard, where he picked up a house brick he found there. Brick in one hand, the Slasher opened the door quietly and stepped inside. In the darkness, he walked down the hall to the front door, opened it and propped it with the brick – just in case he needed to make a quick getaway.

Then it seems he relaxed and spent quite a bit of time in the Howells' home, venturing into several rooms. He slashed a rug on Kevin's bed while he slept and left blood droplets in the bedroom of a younger son. Blood that no doubt came from what had occurred in Coleman's room.

Lesley was asleep, underneath blankets and two overcoats to provide extra warmth on a chilly winter's night. He pulled back the blankets and overcoats and groped her breasts hard enough to leave red marks and bruising. Next he pulled out his razor, sliced her chest four times and then hacked into the blankets and overcoats.

Then, because he claimed he wanted her to wake up, the Slasher closed his hand into a fist and punched the woman several times in the face. Coleman wore dentures, which were shattered by the blow and cut the inside of her mouth. Unconscious, her mouth began to fill with blood, placing her at risk of choking to death.

At this time it seems the Slasher left Coleman and went into the younger boy's room, where he left the spots of blood. The boy awoke and screamed for his parents when he saw a shadowy figure in his room. The man rushed out of the room and down the hall to the front door he'd propped open. Moving the brick, he left it covered in blood, and slammed the door on his way out. Woken by her son's screams May Howell must have been in the hallway at the same time as the Slasher, because she heard the door slam.

She and son Kevin first checked on the boy before entering their guest's room. They were horrified by what they saw; blood covered her face, mouth and chest, with sprays of it on the bedhead and wall behind her. There was also blood sprayed across the venetian blinds in the room and on the bedroom door.

May opened Lesley's mouth to clear away the broken dentures so she didn't swallow them when she regained consciousness. An ambulance was called and Coleman would face weeks of treatment for her broken dentures, damaged jaw and an eye injury.

And the man who did it headed back to his home before the sun came up to avoid the possibility of a milkman or some other early riser spying the blood splatter on his hands and clothing. A home that was just two streets away.

5

"As far as I can ascertain he was well-liked by everybody who knew him."
Brian Doyle trial testimony, September 7, 1959

Six hundred metres away via road, less than half that if someone was to cut through backyards and over fences, lived David Scanlon. Despite being 26 years old, he was still living in the family home in New England Drive, Kingsgrove, with his father Francis Michael and stepmother Jeannie (his mother Ruby had passed away five years earlier).

An L-shaped home – the front door in the nook created by the two legs of the L – it featured the red bricks and tiled roof common in suburbia at the time. It was a small home sitting on a large block with a knee-high red-brick fence out the front, an uncovered driveway and a big backyard. Behind the house was a large triangular park surrounded by houses facing away on all sides. Back fences ringed the park, making it an appealing central access point for someone with a desire to climb into strangers' back yards and then into their homes.

With just two bedrooms, the Scanlon family home would have been a tight fit for three adults. There had been more at one stage. Scanlon had three older siblings. Bessie was born in July 1914, just four months after Francis and Ruby were married. That suggests a forced marriage rather than one created out of love. Scanlon's parents were little more than children themselves; Francis was 18 and Ruby just 15 years old when they were married at St David's in Surry Hills on March 10, 1914.

Two years later Josephine Scanlon was born and then a son, Francis Jr arrived in 1921. That meant at just 23 years of age, Ruby was a mother three times over. And there may be the suggestion that was all the couple planned to have.

Yet eight years later, in timing that speaks to something accidental rather than any planning, David Joseph Scanlon was born in Taree. He was a sickly baby when he came into the world on October 4, 1929, weighing just four pounds – less than a kilogram. Doctors were concerned he would not live long and Scanlon was kept in cotton wool for his early years. While he proved them wrong, he would become quite a highly-strung child and very excitable.

He grew up in the country town of Taree and later Broken Hill, when his father – a railway employee – was transferred there. At about the age of nine, he arrived in Sydney with the family, first living at Paddington and Woollahra before settling into that small home in New England Drive when he was 12.

That small house and the lack of space would make it hard for Scanlon to hide from his father. Family members have said his father was a bully who was violent to both Ruby and Scanlon, which would have the effect of pulling mother and son closer together. A maternal relationship that would end in tragic circumstances one evening when Scanlon was 21. An evening that may hold the origins of the Kingsgrove Slasher.

6

"I called out to my father and he wouldn't believe me and he just told me to go back to sleep."
Anne Willis committal hearing testimony, June 18, 1959

The violence meted out in the guest bedroom of the Howell home didn't satisfy the Slasher's urges for long. After striking so close to his own home, four days later he returned to the neighbouring suburb of Beverly Hills where he had committed some of his first attacks and perhaps felt a little more comfortable.

He crossed the train lines that were responsible for steady growth of the area, what was then referred to generically as "the western suburbs". He headed in the direction of where the M5 today cuts along the southern edge of Canterbury golf course, stopping at the top end of Tallawalla Street. Beyond a preference for homes close to parks or scrubland to help camouflage his getaway, there is very little information about how he chose where he would use his razor. He would insist to police that he never picked out any of his victims ahead of time, never did any reconnaissance on them. He hadn't seen them out and about during the day, liked the way they looked and then followed them home. Instead he gave the impression that the homes were chosen effectively at random, that he kept climbing inside to look around and only brought the razor out when he realised there were suitable female targets asleep in their beds.

If that's the case, then it made the attack on Anne Willis all the more disturbing. For Anne was just seven years old but that didn't stop him from using the razor on her. On Wednesday, July 18, Anne went to bed at 7 o'clock. Her parents Marjory and Allen would stay up until around 10pm. Almost three hours later, the Slasher was in their backyard.

He'd found an open window but it was too high to get to from the ground. In the Willis' yard he found an old cane chair and placed it underneath the bathroom window. In the darkness, he quietly removed the flyscreen, leaving it leaning against the side of the house, pushed the window open and gained entry. With daylight still hours away, he took his time in the family's house. But the first thing he did before wandering through the rooms was unlock the back door and prop it open which made for an easier escape route than trying to make his way out through the bathroom window.

After creeping through the house, he made his way to Marjory and Allen's bedroom. He watched them sleep for a short while before pulling a razor from his pocket and slashing their blankets. That would have been enough to let them know the Slasher had been in their house. But it wasn't enough for him; and so he went into the room of seven-year-old Anne. He slashed at her blankets, then used the razor to cut a gash through her pajamas, near her chest. Anne woke up when he began pulling and tugging at her pajama top. Seeing a dark figure in her room, she screamed out.

"Daddy! There is a man in my room!"

Night Terrors

"You're alright pet, go back to sleep," her father called from his bed, thinking she was having a nightmare.

A terrible minute or two passed in silence before Anne screamed in terror again, by which time the Slasher had left her room and run out the back door. If her father had risen when she first called, he may have come face to face with the Slasher in the darkened hallway of his own house.

At that second scream, Allen jumped out of bed and ran into her room. He swept Anne up in his arms and brought her back to Marjory in their bed. Then Allen searched the house for the man, starting with her bedroom. Turning on the light he saw Anne's slashed blankets – and then he called the police.

It wasn't until the police arrived that the family realised the razor had been used on Anne as well. Miraculously she herself had not been cut but when the policeman took a look at her he found the long gash in her pajama top running from the area of her left breast down towards her waist. While Anne had been left without any physical scars from the attack, it would cause the seven-year-old a lot of mental terror over the next few years.

The inspection of Anne by the police could suggest they had started to join the dots, had begun to realise there was a man out there breaking into houses armed with a razor. Likely they thought there might have been just three attacks; discounting the first on Campbell because it happened in a car and not a house.

While things may have been falling in place for the police, the attacks still hadn't popped up on the radar of the city's newspaper reporters. Neither the violence of the assault on Coleman or the young age of the victim in the latest outrage appeared in the newspapers the next day. A search through *The Sun* and *The Mirror* – the two afternoon tabloids fighting for readers' eyeballs – the day after those crimes yielded not a single story. But the tipping point would be reached with the fifth attack, on a 12-year-old girl; not long afterwards an unknown journalist would come up with a name for the man – The Kingsgrove Slasher.

7

"A pervert who slashes the bedclothes of sleeping women was abroad again in the Kingsgrove area last night."
Daily Mirror, July 28, 1956

Kingsgrove wasn't the only Sydney suburb dealing with a problem prowler in 1956. In Carlingford just northeast of Parramatta a group of men armed themselves with rifles, shotguns and clubs and formed a vigilante group to spend the night hunting a nasty piece of work.

According to the *Sydney Morning Herald,* in May 1956, the suburb was terrorised by "a heavily built prowler carrying a double-barrelled shotgun". In the first few days of that month, he had knocked out one resident in his backyard, smashed windows of other homes, pointed his gun at home owners and, perhaps least alarmingly, "wrecked gardens and stolen poultry and gardening tools from backyard".

The five men who made up that posse agreed to pose for a *Herald* photographer and ended up on the front page. According to the gang leader Bruce Faux, they were just protecting "their womenfolk and children". He also claimed to have had his very own run-in with the armed prowler.

"Last night I heard a noise in the backyard and went outside," Faux said. "He threatened me with his gun, then clouted me down. I landed in the dirt and he fled. I called a few of the boys to help me but we didn't catch him."

"When I went back I found one of my windows broken." How could the head vigilante expect to protect the whole neighbourhood when he couldn't even take care of his own backyard?

Vigilante groups would start forming in and around Kingsgrove soon enough but the more immediate change was the newspapers waking up to what was happening. The afternoon tabloids – as is the case with tabloids today – ran big on crime, so it's a little surprising it wasn't until the fifth Slasher break-in that they sent their prowl cars over to the suburb.

It was the attack on 12-year-old Gloria Geyson that changed things. The girl lived at the southern end of Armitree Street, in a home that no longer exists because it sat in the path of the M5.

It was a Friday night – July 27 – and with no school the next morning, Gloria stayed up until 11.30pm before falling into the clutches of sleep, her bedroom window left slightly ajar despite it being the middle of winter. She was roused around 5am when she felt what she took to be her mother Dorothy pulling at her clothes. She rolled over and instead of her mother, she saw what she assumed to be her father Reg.

"Da-aad," she said sleepily, reaching out with her hand to touch his face. That was when he tilted his head slightly to take her thumb into his mouth. And so she screamed.

The man ran out, spilling several razor blades on her bed. Reg, responding to his daughter's cry, rushed into her room. She told him what had happened; he raced for the back door to see if he could find the mysterious figure. Gloria got up and headed to the kitchen, turning on all the lights as she went. When her father returned, he noticed the slashes across the chest of her pajama top, singlet and slip. He was relieved to find she hadn't been cut herself but a later look at Gloria's bed found the blanket and overcoat she had been sleeping under were cut.

Soon her parents ventured outside, where they found a garbage bin had been placed under Gloria's bedroom window. The edges of the flyscreen had been nailed to the window frame but the screen itself had been ripped out. Reg went back inside and called the police.

The next morning Dorothy would find those three Gillette Blue brand razors in Gloria's bed and spot the droplets of blood the Slasher had left behind. That afternoon, three papers ran stories about the events in Armitree Street, each complete with salacious headlines. "Hunt for sex fiend" screamed the *Sydney Truth*, "Slasher attacks at dawn", trumpeted *The Sun*, while *The Mirror* went all the way with "Sex slasher attacks girl in bedroom". The following day the *Sunday Telegraph* joined the party with "Sex maniac's razor attack in bedroom". Even interstate papers – including the *Melbourne Argus* – were intrigued enough to give the story at least a few paragraphs of space.

The story in the *Truth* was uncannily similar to *The Mirror*'s coverage, right down to the quotes from 37-year-old Reg Geyson. Someone at the paper had obviously ducked down to the newsagents to pick up a first edition of *The Mirror* and then bashed together "their" story. The *Sunday Telegraph* story a day later seemed to have been compiled via the same method.

The Mirror had the jump on everyone else. They were likely the only paper to bother driving out to Kingsgrove to see if the family wanted to talk – as it turned out Reg was happy for a chat.

The Mirror's story – which called the attacker a "sex maniac" and a "pervert" – labelled this the fourth attack in three weeks (the Campbell slashing had still not been linked to the Slasher).

Reg told *The Mirror*'s readers about the early morning raid where his daughter awoke to discover "the pervert crouched over her bed wielding his razor" (*The Mirror*'s words, not his).

"It's pretty horrible to think this maniac could just have easily have cut Gloria's throat," Reg said.

"He was pretty shrewd because he got in through a window and then opened all the doors he was going to use to leave the house."

Detective-Sergeant Wedlock at Kogarah police station was put in charge of the investigation. It would prove to be a thankless job – three years would pass before the police had their man. Before that happened, he would go on to find his way into the bedrooms of at least 13 other women and girls.

8

"The district has been in a high state of tension because a pervert has already entered three homes."
Daily Mirror, July 31, 1956

When it came to solving the case, the police were really on a hiding to nothing. For starters, Kingsgrove didn't even have a police station. In the suburb the presence of the boys in blue was limited to a small three-square-metre callbox on Kingsgrove Road, immediately south of the train station. It was staffed by two constables who had a motorcycle and sidecar for patrols (it would be replaced by a patrol car the following year). Presumably, if they were on patrol and someone rang for help, the call would go unanswered – hardly an ideal situation when one is looking to catch a serial prowler.

On top of that, they had no idea of who they were looking for. They were searching in the dark without so much as even a vague description of what the man looked like. While Anne Willis, Marlene Storz and Gloria Geyson had all seen the Slasher, none were able to give police a physical description.

To them he was a shadowy nightmare figure that simply appeared next to their bed. He did leave several razor blades behind at the Geyson house; if they were ever checked for fingerprints, they must have returned nothing for there is no record of the prints. While he left his blood at the scene of the Geyson crime DNA analysis was several decades away. At any rate DNA is really only useful when you already have a suspect. Five attacks in and the police pretty much had nothing to go on.

What would be a further pain for police throughout the three-year investigation was a number of women and girls who falsely claimed to be a victim of the Slasher. Newspaper coverage of the late 1950s was littered with the claims of women who insisted they were attacked by the Slasher but whose claims were quickly dismissed by police.

At the trial in September 1959, Detective Sergeant Brian Doyle (the man who would crack the case) seemed to express sympathy towards the accused for the weight of these false accusations. In language that sounds harsh to modern ears, he said it had "became fashionable" for women to say they were victims of the Slasher.

He said "...consequently the police department was inundated with frivolous and flimsy reports from nervous and neurotic women, that they had been attacked. A lot of them even displayed minor self-inflicted wounds on their faces and breasts."

The women's actions, he said, were encouraged by newspapers, which would give them their 15 minutes of fame in print as a Slasher victim even before the police had decided whether there was anything to their claims.

The claims of other women to have had run-ins with the Slasher started immediately after the Geyson attack was splashed in the afternoon tabloids. Over the next few days, there would be three stories of different incidents, each attributed to the Slasher. The day after the Geyson attack, *The Mirror* carried the story of a Mrs Maureen Graham, who lived in Morgan Street, Kingsgrove. She claimed that she was awoken by the noise a prowler made while removing a flyscreen. She crept into her mother's bedroom and then the pair returned to Graham's room, switched on the light and scared the prowler away.

On the Monday night along Moorefields Road 15-year-old Maureen Steel woke screaming, claiming she'd seen the silhouette of a man trying to get into her bedroom window. *The Sun*, which had already decided it was none other than the "mad sex pervert" who had been "terrorising Kingsgrove families", wrote that he ran off through a nearby cemetery. "Just let me get my hands on this chap," her father told *The Sun*, "I'll guarantee he won't do any more prowling." *The Mirror* was a bit more skeptical, pointing out that Detective Wedlock was not able to find any sign that someone had been outside her window.

On Tuesday, July 31, police responded to a call from a "hysterical woman" (the *Daily Mirror*'s words) who thought the "Kingsgrove pervert" was in her backyard. *The Sun* went for the beat-up, claiming the Slasher had "escaped capture by seconds", while later stating the reason for the woman's call was because she heard "scratching" outside. The paper also bizarrely suggested residents in Kingsgrove knew him as "the man with the leering face"; more likely only *The Sun* ever called him that. Especially given that no-one had actually *seen* his face.

Up to this point the Slasher had shown little trouble in getting inside people's homes undetected; even walking around inside for a time. Yet here were three instances in as many days where he was so clumsy that he couldn't even get the window open without waking his victims. If these women saw anyone at all outside – and it seems highly likely two of them didn't see anyone – it certainly wasn't the Kingsgrove Slasher.

It does seem the press coverage prompted a change in the police investigation. After being in charge for just a few days, Detective Wedlock saw the case handed over to the Criminal Investigation Branch (CIB). Press reports claimed extra police had been made available to quickly respond to any reports of the Slasher. Some of those police were making life tough for men spotted on the street after sundown. "Dozens of men have been questioned when found walking the darkened streets of Kingsgrove," *The Sun* reported. "Many of them have been shift workers and all have been able to give a satisfactory explanation of their actions."

The heightened police activity and sudden media attention seemed to cause the Slasher to break stride a little. After assaulting four females in July, he slowed things down for a few weeks. His next crime would occur in the early hours of August 15 in a house in Kirrang Street, Beverly Hills, which today has been cleaved in two by the four lanes of the M5 toll road. The house in question, where the Nicholls family lived in the late 1950s, now pushes up against the noise embankment on the southern side.

The crime he would commit in that house would be the only one of the 18 charges he would face in 1959 that listed a male name as the victim. That name was Noel Nicholls – as the man of the house (it's the 1950s, remember) he owned the empty bed in their baby daughter's room that the Slasher attacked with his razor.

But it could have easily been his wife Dora who was the victim. Or even their one-year-old daughter, Kim. At midnight Kim woke up and wouldn't settle, so Dora dragged herself out of bed to see what was the matter. Finally, to try and get her daughter back to sleep, Dora lay down on the room's spare bed, situated under the window. She dozed off for half an hour before waking up, realising where she was and rejoining Noel in their own bed.

Ninety minutes later, at 2am on Wednesday, Dora was woken by the sound of the venetian blinds in Kim's bedroom banging in the breeze. That seemed strange as, when they all went to bed, the window had been left only slightly ajar. When Noel went to investigate, he noticed the window had been opened as far as possible and the flyscreen removed. Then he looked at the bed beneath the window – where Dora had been sleeping just over an hour ago – and saw the sheets and pillow had been slashed. Worried, he checked on Kim, who was unharmed.

When he was confessing to his other crimes in 1959, the Slasher would say he never entered the baby's room; he'd just lent in over the window sill, gave the razor a workout and then left. He told police the slashed empty bed was to serve as a reminder that he was still around. Perhaps he was irritated by the fake Slasher incidents getting all the attention.

2

*"Police regard the increased crime rate as serious, but have had no
difficulty in controlling it."*
CIB Superintendent Calman, *Sydney Morning Herald*, May 2,
1956

There is the belief today that the 1950s was a more innocent
time, where the only crime committed was in the city, by
professional crims. The suburbs, by comparison, were
bastions of peace and harmony where everyone felt so secure they
could leave their doors unlocked and their windows open without a
care in the world.

While it is true some people did leave doors and windows
unlocked, it seems something more born of complacency than
anything else. Even during the two peaks of the Kingsgrove
Slasher's run he was still finding doors unlocked and windows left
open. Everyone knew some guy armed with a razor was walking
around at night breaking into houses and still some home owners
didn't feel the need to lock up at night.

In the late 1950s, suburban crime – including murder – was not
unusual. It's worth taking a diversion to see that, while the

Kingsgrove Slasher was on his reign of terror, it wasn't as though he was the sole blemish on an otherwise spotless suburban landscape. In February 1955, Elsie Muriel Berry shot her husband Charles in their Earlwood home. That afternoon Charles had dragged her along to two separate pubs and gotten drunk while she didn't touch a drop.

When they got home, he threatened to choke her before pulling out a sawn-off rifle and said he would shoot her. She waited until he fell asleep cradling the rifle and then took it from him. Charged with murder, the prosecution said she pointed the gun at him and pulled the trigger while she insisted it had gone off accidentally while she was holding it as she leant over the bed to see if Charles was asleep. After half an hour the jury returned a verdict of not guilty.

April 1955 saw Moya Ann Norris take a carving knife and stab her husband Reginald through the heart. She claimed she had acted in self-defence as he had assaulted her that night and many others. "My husband was berserk and in a mad rage," she told the court of that night. Ninety minutes after it retired, the jury found her not guilty.

In Strathfield 57-year-old Dorothy Haug, a housemistress at Meriden School was found battered to death in her room in August of the same year. Three months later Charles James Smith was judged to be insane and unable to stand trial for her murder.

In December 1955 new mother, 20-year-old Freda Walsh, was placed on a good behavior bond after trying to kill her three-week-old son Brian. She admitted she had given him two morphine sulphate tablets with the intent to murder him.

Still in 1955, Fred Brandy, a 23-year-old welder stabbed his stepfather Charles Lloyd in the chest at Kingsford. Lloyd had attacked his wife and then went after Brandy, armed with a carving knife. Brandy picked up a vegetable knife while running from his stepdad, but ended up killing him.

In January 1956 in Beverly Hills, Leo Ogelsneft battered his 72-year-old mother to death with a bottle of lemonade. He placed her body on a bed, saturated it with kerosene and then tried to set her on fire. As the flames took hold, Ogelsneft – a doctor from Russia – stabbed himself with a carving knife. Police were told he had become depressed after his wife divorced him and he could not get a job as a doctor in NSW.

A Dee Why home owner in March 1956 used a gun to try and get a boarder to leave his home. Albert Fowler had been renting a room in 75-year-old Frederick Ekman's house for more than two years. Ekman wanted to sell the house and kept asking him to leave but Fowler had refused. He had taken to locking his bedroom door to protect himself from the landlord. One evening, Ekman knocked on the door and when Fowler drew near, he fired two shots through it. They just missed Fowler's head. When police arrived, they found Ekman had four loaded guns; "if those guns had not jammed you would be arresting me for murder," he told police. Somehow the landlord was acquitted of attempted murder.

A 19-year-old by the name of Peter McGrath was sentenced to four years jail in July 1956 for glassing someone at a Parramatta taxi rank. The Merrylands teen had smashed a beer bottle and jabbed its jagged edge into his victim's neck.

A Marrickville woman had a total of 20 stitches in her leg, arm and head after being slashed with an ice pick while in a telephone booth. In February 1957, Enid Rackstraw was calling her husband; while on the phone a "New Australian" (1950s code for migrant) banged on the door and told her to hurry. When she ignored him, he opened the door, dragged her out by the throat and slashed her with the ice pick.

Night Terrors

In October 1958 a 27-year-old Earlwood man was convicted over the rape of a 15-year-old girl. The pair were in his car at the national park when he threatened to "turn the girl loose to the dingoes" unless she agreed to sex. She refused and left the car only to hear dingo howls in the darkness (they were the man's friends hiding in the bush). She returned to the car where "intimacy then occurred" according to the demure news coverage in the *Sydney Morning Herald*. The man claimed the girl gave her consent and anyway, he thought she was 16.

Something strange happened at Girrahween Park in Earlwood on October 20, 1958. Two girls aged 11 and 12 were walking through the park at 6.30pm when a man approached them with a knife. He put the knife on the ground in front of the pair and started talking to them. The more brazen of the pair simply picked up the knife, chucked it into bushland and ran away. This happened at the tail-end of a long break for the Slasher, otherwise police might have thought it was him because his second batch of crimes would be committed in this area.

Police in Burwood in May 1959 were looking for a man dubbed the "polite prowler", because he was well-mannered and dressed in a grey suit. He had attacked a sleeping nurse at a Summer Hill hospital earlier that month. On May 10 he tried his luck with four different women, failing each time. He ran from a teenage girl's bedroom when she shone a torch in his face, attempted to reach through an old woman's door and remove the chain on the inside, was chased away after being spotted trying to get into the nurse's quarters at the Masonic Hospital in Ashfield and then was found in the bedroom of a female doctor. When asked what he was doing there he said he was "looking for Jack Frost". Then he politely left.

And this stuff was all going on around the same time the Kingsgrove Slasher was at work.

10

"Women and girls are barricading themselves in at night in fear of the Kingsgrove Slasher."
Sydney Morning Herald, August 19, 1956

Later, the Slasher would insist that he did not know any of his victims, did not pick them out ahead of time. What happened just three nights after he cut up the bed in the Nicholls house, when he was standing over the sleeping form of a 16-year-old girl named Annette Gurney, calls that into question.

He had to know her, had to at least have seen her before. She lived on New England Drive with her parents and 10-year-old brother Dennis, just five doors down from his own home. A teen who had just left high school and had started at business school while the Slasher was in his late 20s, it's unlikely they were on speaking terms – perhaps however, he'd met her parents. She lived slightly closer to the station than he did; he would have to pass her house each day on the kilometre-long walk to catch his train to the city each morning. He may have even seen her out and about on the weekends. There is really no way she could have been completely unknown to him. And what went on in that bedroom suggests that she could have been different to all the other women.

Annette's house was similar to his own; red-brick, tiled roof, small brick fence out the front, big yard out the back. And he'd been in both the yard and the house. In fact, the Slasher would go on to tell police he'd been inside almost every house in that street.

At around 4am, he was in the Gurneys' yard. Grabbing a bucket, he upturned it and placed it under Annette's window. For a man who claimed he'd never he'd picked out the women ahead of time, he seemed to make a habit of climbing through *their* bedroom window rather than the windows of any male members of the household. He cut out the wire screen in the window and pushed it up (Annette had left it open slightly because her room was stuffy).

Once inside, he moved a chair containing some of Annette's clothing. He picked up one of the teen's bras and slashed it through with his razor. Then he headed to Annette's bed which was pushed up against a wall. He sliced into her pajama top with five slashes before cutting into her blankets and bed sheets as well.

Annette, sleeping on her side facing the wall, was disturbed by the sound a man panting very close to her. Rolling over, she saw a figure crouching over her. She watched as the figure straightened up and moved towards the window as if to check whether he had been seen.

Sleepy Annette thought it was her father Reg. Until the shadow turned back from the window and headed towards her bed and she caught a glimpse of his face via the glow from a streetlight shining through her window. Then she screamed, which sent the Slasher back to the window; with one hand on the sill, he sprang out in a single movement.

That moment where the Slasher walked to the window to check to see if the coast was clear before turning back indicates that he wasn't quite finished with the 16-year-old. Perhaps this indicates that he did know her, that he had planned something special.

Detective Sergeant Doyle certainly thought so. During questioning after the capture he would suggest the Slasher had planned to inflict serious injuries on Annette. The man's response was nothing more than "I can't say". It's a response of a man not at all keen to admit what really lay beneath the surface. In the questioning he remembered where Gurney lived, remembered she was one of his earlier attacks and even what he did with the razor. But as for his plans after that point, he can't say.

Upon hearing Annette's yell Reg rushed into her bedroom. She told her father what had happened and he rushed to the window in case he could spy the invader.

The city's four main newspapers were all interested in Annette's story. *The Mirror* even ran a photo of dressing-gown clad Annette, sleep-tousled dark hair, manicured eyebrows and an uncertain smile on her face, holding a blanket with several slashes plainly visible (a day later, she ensured she was done up when the *Herald*'s photographer came calling). *The Mirror*'s journalist managed to speak to her just an hour after the Slasher had left her bedroom.

"I thought it was daddy as he often comes in and sees that the window is shut," she told the reporter.

"But this was quick breathing, like panting, and I turned over and saw a man standing there by my bed, just staring. He moved quickly to the window as if to jump out then came back alongside the bed.

"I was too scared to do a thing. He stared at me and I could see him quite plainly in the reflection of a streetlight coming in my window."

The police got two things from the Gurney household that they'd not gotten elsewhere. One was a palm print; the Slasher had left one behind as he vaulted out the window (there would also be court testimony about a fingerprint being lifted off a bathroom tile in the Willis house but there is no sign of it in the court documents).

The second thing was a description of the Slasher; Annette had gotten a good look at him thanks to that streetlight. She told police her attacker was aged between 20 and 25, was well-built and had a mop of wavy hair. Though it's odd that she didn't recognise that it was the same man who lived just a few doors away.

Another thing emerged from the Gurney incident – an agreed-upon name for the attacker. Before this point, the papers had called the attacker a range of names: sex maniac, pervert, maniacal sex pervert, mad sex pervert or the Kingsgrove prowler. It was *The Sun* that struck the name the "Kingsgrove Slasher" after the Nicholls crime, but it took a few days to stick; by the time of the Gurney attack all the papers had adopted that name.

11

"Gunmen wait for Slasher"
Daily Mirror, August 24, 1956

There they were, on page two of *The Daily Mirror* dated August 24. Arthur Jackson, 28, and his younger brother Rex. Arthur's face is an oval while Rex's is more angular but their identical receding hairlines and widow's peaks mark them out as siblings.

While Rex is wearing a collared shirt and trousers, Arthur has curiously opted for a dressing gown, pyjamas and slippers (perhaps at the request of the photographer). The most striking part of the image is the rifles they cradle in their arms.

Just two days earlier a prowler had tried to get into the brothers' Wolli Street home they shared with their respective wives and children. After arriving home late, Rex was settling their 13-month-old boy down to bed while his wife (in a sign that the 1950s really were a different time) was in the kitchen setting the table for breakfast. "I heard a rattle at the back door but didn't take much notice," she said.

"The noise got louder and I realised it was someone trying to get into the house."

She screamed and ran to Rex, while he went for his gun. Which wasn't where he left it. In an explanation that suggested Rex just left his gun and live ammunition lying around the place, his wife said she had "cleaned up" the day before and "put the gun and bullets out of the way".

By the time Rex had laid his hands on the rifle and loaded it, the prowler had gone. Yet he still sat up all night cradling a loaded weapon, just in case he returned.

Of course, the Jacksons and the papers immediately assumed it was the Kingsgrove Slasher, even though the coppers managed to catch the culprit less than 300 metres away. And it wasn't the Slasher but a 28-year-old spring maker.

Albert John Byrnes would appear at Kogarah Court of Petty Sessions the same day charged with having been found unlawfully in the Jacksons' backyard. The prowler's wife had left him and he'd told police he'd gone into their yard because he "had an urge to see a woman in bed".

The magistrate EJ Etherton fined Byrnes £5. Showing some awareness of the Jacksons' suburban arsenal, he also advised Byrnes that wandering around people's backyards in Kingsgrove could lead to being shot.

The heightened police presence in the suburb, and the community's sudden focus on finding the Kingsgrove Slasher should have seen peeping Toms, prowlers and the like find another suburb to ply their trade. But it didn't. At the same time Byrnes was nabbed police also caught another prowler in Gloucester Road, Hurstville, where the suburb rubbed up against Kingsgrove.

Detective Sergeants Allan Neal and Stan North had just wrapped up a fruitless night patrolling for the Slasher when they spied a man with a blue handkerchief covering his face bank-robber style. He was walking out the gate of one Mrs Minnie Morgan, who had just scared him away by switching on an outside light.

Police chased the man down and arrested him. He was a Thomas Millwood, a 22-year-old labourer from Arncliffe. Just to be on the safe side, the police organised a line-up and brought in several of the Slasher's victims to see if Millwood was their man. He wasn't.

Another Gloucester Road resident, Mrs Mear told *The Mirror* (and any prowler who read the paper) that her husband worked nights and she was home alone.

"I sleep with a piece of iron piping beside the bed," she said. "What a nightmare this has been; every visitor or any little noise has made me a bag of nerves.

"There are quite a few women whose husbands work night shifts, and all of them are too frightened to open the door at night."

With the increased public fears of the Slasher in the Kingsgrove area those armed Jackson men weren't the only ones looking to take some sort of action. Suburban fathers started arranging street patrols to try and catch the man themselves.

"Several men will take it in turns to patrol homes in our street," said David Jones, incorrectly identified by *The Sun* as the father of one of the Slasher's first victims. "They'll be relieved after a couple of hours.

"This man is getting gamer and gamer as he goes undetected. Many mothers in this street are terror-stricken. They fear he will eventually kill someone."

The Sun didn't identify what street the dads were patrolling but a piece in *The Mirror* the following day about a new vigilante group did. They would be patrolling New England Drive, the very street the Slasher lived in.

12

"Police raided several homes today in an effort to capture the sex-crazed Kingsgrove razor slasher"
Daily Mirror, October 29, 1956

Every journalist has their go-to sources, especially on a long-running story. They're the people the journo knows are always willing to offer some comment, willing to speak on the record without the need to spend any time being persuaded. They can just get the source on the phone, shoot some questions at them and get the words they need – all in a matter of minutes. Very handy in a job that has daily deadlines.

When it comes to the Slasher's victims his next one, Valerie Thompson, would fill that role. She was easily the most approachable, the most willing to fill a reporter's notebook with quotes or stand in front of a news reporter's camera flash. Some of the women understandably shied away from talking to the media about their experience – either at the time or during the court case (though they weren't able to avoid the camera flash outside the court house).

Valerie Thompson wasn't like that. Just hours after the Slasher stood in her bedroom watching her sleep next to husband Ron, Valerie posed for two newspaper photographers. During the court hearings, she was there again for the press, offering quotes about the sentencing and posing for more photos. Even the Slasher noticed this; "I remember her particularly well," he told Detective Sgt Doyle. "She had had her photo in the paper several times."

After a spate of six attacks in two months, the Slasher appeared to put his feet up and take a break. He'd stepped inside the Gurney home in the early hours of August 18 but the razor wouldn't reappear until just past midnight on the last Monday in October, back in Beverly Hills again.

That didn't stop reporters keen for some Slasher copy from suggesting the man in a bedroom of two young women in Bexley was him, despite nothing being cut. "Police believe the intruder entered through an unlocked door," *The Mirror* wrote. Which did beg the question why, with seven women just a suburb away finding the Slasher in their bedrooms in the dead of night, were people still forgetting to lock up before going to bed?

That was a question Ron Thompson may have asked himself some time on the morning of Monday, October 29. He and hiw wife Valerie had had visitors over that weekend at their home in Elouera Street, Beverly Hills (the street is now cut in two by the M5) and spent some time entertaining in the sunroom on the Sunday. A window in that room at the back of the house had been opened at some stage in the afternoon.

Night Terrors

When Ron walked around the house before he and Valerie went to bed he locked the doors and saw all the windows were down and, he assumed, locked. But that sunroom window hadn't been locked, and that was the window the Slasher climbed through just after midnight.

He propped the back door open with a brick, then walked down the hall and into the Thompsons' bedroom, passing their baby in a bassinet sleeping just outside their door. A short time thereafter, Valerie woke and saw a figure leaning over the bed.

"Wake up! There's a man in the room!" she screamed.

Leaping out of bed, Ron chased the Slasher out of the room and saw him bump into the baby's bassinet, causing it to spin around but thankfully not flip over. Valerie got up and called the police while Ron chased the man into the backyard and watching him jump a side fence and run off into scrubland, which would later become a golf course. Ron returned to the house and there he noticed the blood staining the right arm of Valerie's pajama coat. The coat and clothing underneath had been slashed, with a razor cutting all the way through to the skin. Rolling the clothes back, they saw the inch-long cut at her elbow. Additionally, all the buttons of Valerie's pajamas top had been cut off.

Later that night Thompson showed off the small bandage on her arm in *The Sun*, which oddly referred to the incident as the Slasher's "fourth attack on a young mother". None of the seven previous attacks were on a mother, and four of them featured victims aged 16 or under. "I don't think I'll ever sleep until they catch this maniac," she said.

The Mirror got a photo of Valerie holding out the blood-spattered sleeve of her pajama top. The reporter also got the scoop that police raided a house at St Peters looking for a man who had been arrested a year earlier for breaking into the Thompsons' house.

He was able to convince police he hadn't been back since, that he wasn't the Slasher and hadn't cut Valerie.

The Thompson house seemed a magnet for criminals. According to *The Mirror* story, there had been four incidents over the previous 18 months. In March 1955, in an eerie coincidence, a man crept into her bedroom and slashed open her pajama top. Six weeks after that Valerie saw a peeping Tom peering through a window. In July 1956 a neighbour chased away another peeper watching Valerie while hiding in bushes at the back of the house. Then, a few weeks before the Slasher visit, they woke to the sounds of a burglar riffling through their things.

The couple kept hearing noises outside their house at night in the following weeks. There was the sound of milk bottles being knocked over on the front porch and, another time, sheets of corrugated iron down near their back fence started rattling.

It wasn't their imagination – it was the Slasher come to pay them a few more visits. It seemed being chased by Ron had sent a thrill through him and, like a kid plinking pebbles against a window to get someone's attention, he shook iron and knocked over milk bottles to get Ron's attention.

".. I went back there a few times in the next few weeks," he would explain during police questioning. "I made just enough noises to get the husband to come out and chase me again. I made noises in the side passage and rattled on the windows."

But there would be no more chasing; Ron would come outside when he heard the noises but never be able to find anyone. For all the Slasher's efforts and noise-making, he didn't seem brave enough to actually show himself to Ron.

13

"Terror has gripped the Kingsgrove-Beverly Hills district and residents are once again living behind locked doors."
The Sun, October 29, 1956

Exactly a month before the Thompson assault there was a big change in the life of David Scanlon of New England Drive, Kingsgrove – he got married.

Scanlon would make the trip up north to the Gloucester area – north of Newcastle and about an hour west of Taree, where he grew up – to visit one of his sisters. It was on one of these trips in late 1954 that Scanlon met a dark-haired 20-year-old by the name of Jean Doreen Garland.

Things moved swiftly for the couple; just six months after they met David proposed to her and she accepted. Perhaps they bonded quickly over a shared understanding of lost mothers. Jean was just one when her mother Agnes died, most likely while giving birth to her youngest, Nancy (Jean also had an older sibling in Thomas). Her father Ernest, either unable or unwilling to look after his children (he and Agnes never married) had them put in homes.

David had lost his mother Ruby far more recently; just three years before he and Jean first met. On the night of August 24, 1951, David came home to Kingsgrove from his job in the city doing clerical work for an importer. Walking into the darkened house he tripped over the body of his mother lying dead on the floor. On August 28 an obituary ran in the *Sydney Morning Herald*.

"Ruby Scanlon, August 24, 1951, at her residence [in] New England Drive, Kingsgrove. Beloved wife of Francis Scanlon and dear mother of Bessie, Josie, Frank and David."

She was 52 years old. Scanlon's sisters noticed a change in David after his mother died. An excitable boy who had grown into a chatty young man eager to share his news with the family, David became withdrawn after Ruby's death. One sister, who had been seeing a Dr Listwan for a "minor nervous disorder" in 1953 expressed concern for David's health. She told Dr Listwan he was quiet, always stayed at home and his actions were "slow". She tried to get him to visit the doctor, but David wouldn't have any of it. It was a mood that perhaps was exacerbated when his father found someone to replace Ruby – a woman named Jeannie. She moved into Frank's New England Drive home and into his bed as well. All while son David – always his mother's son – slept under the same roof.

Maybe two lonely people in David and Jean had found each other. Around 12 months after their engagement, on September 29, 1956, the couple were married at St Stephens Church of England in Newtown. A month later they would move in together; living in a boarding house on the north side of the harbour in Waiwera Street, Lavender Bay.

But the work of the Slasher would continue.

14

"She cried out in fright 'what do you want?'."
Daily Mirror, November 26, 1956

So there he was, outside Rosalie Meyer's house just after 3am on November 26. It was a Monday but he didn't seem too concerned about the need to have to go to work in a few hours. He seldom did – for a night crawler with a day job the Slasher would commit a staggering number of his crimes on weeknights.

Of the 18 crimes he would admit to just three were committed on a Saturday, and none on a Sunday. Bearing in mind all but one of his assaults – the first, against Margaret Campbell – were committed after the hands on the clock had passed midnight, that means heading out on a Friday or a Saturday night to prowl for hours on end was his *least* popular option.

He preferred weeknights; his favourite day for attacks was Wednesday. Eight of his victims woke up to find him inside their houses early on Wednesday mornings. While everyone else was going to bed because they had to be up for work or school the next day, he didn't feel the need. Maybe that they *were* home was the whole point; a weeknight increased the chances someone would be inside when he chose to peer through a window or test a door knob to see if it had been left unlocked. A weeknight would also be unlikely to offer up the risk of running into a group of drunken men walking home.

So there he was outside the 18-year-old Rosalie's home in Bayview Avenue, Undercliffe (now the eastern edge of Earlwood), which was several suburbs east of his usual Kingsgrove stomping ground. The home certainly wasn't chosen because of its ease of access. It was situated on a downhill section of the road that had been carved through rock. That rock was what Rosalie's house was perched on, meaning it sat at least six metres above street level. Though the Slasher likely chose to access the house from the rear, where the back fence passed just metres from a walking track.

It had been a warm weekend, with Sunday temperatures nudging 30 degrees. The heat hung around for the start of the working week, which was why Rosalie had left her window open when she went to sleep. Instead of a cooling breeze coming through that window, it was the Slasher.

He climbed into her room so quietly that she did not stir. It gave him the chance to look around her room, as though he was searching for something. Apparently not finding what he was looking for, the Slasher climbed back out the window and went into the backyard of the house. That's where he found a 60-centimetre length of hardwood and took it with him back to her room. He later claimed the intent had been to use the wood to prop open the front door of the house as he had done previously, but the Slasher would end up using it for something far worse.

Back in the room, he didn't head to the front door with the block of wood but stayed near the sleeping woman. His razor cut the pull cord attached to the ceiling light so the girl in the bed couldn't turn it on should she wake up. The Slasher then took to the bedding with the razor before cutting into Rosalie's pajamas, slicing the buttons off her top.

Then the Slasher took the block of wood and hit her across the head. The pain woke the teen up and he must have kept hitting her because she had defence wounds across her hands and knuckles, as though she had been warding off blows.

She would only vaguely remember being hit with the wood but what happened next would be firmly etched in her mind. She felt someone was groping her breasts quite painfully and growling like a dog. Seeing a figure at her bedside, she screamed and the growling figure fled out the window.

Her mother heard Rosalie cry out but initially dismissed it as a recurrence of nightmares she once had; where she would scream out in terror but have no recollection of it the next day. However, just to make sure everything was alright, she headed to Rosalie's bedroom.

"What is the matter Rosalie?" she asked as soon as she opened the door. He daughter staggered towards her and, as she came closer, the light thrown into the room from the hallway highlighted the blood trickling from a head wound. A wound that would require five stitches and a three-day stay in Marrickville Hospital; but the mother would tell a court several years later than the Slasher's assault left more lasting scars than the one across her forehead.

The newspaper reports of the Meyer assault highlighted what is to modern eyes, a creepy aspect of the Slasher coverage. *The Mirror*'s headline screamed "Pretty girl bashed" and described her as a "pretty teenager" in the opening paragraph. A previous victim, 16-year-old Annette Gurney had been described as "pretty" and "attractive". The next victim – a 14-year-old girl – would be described the same way.

It obviously didn't raise an eyebrow in the conservative 1950s but really, having adult male reporters describing teenage victims of sexual assault as "pretty" is unsettling. It's as though there's a tabloid effort to titillate the reader as well as shock them.

The coverage – which included no interviews or photo of anyone from the Meyer family – also showed no-one really had any idea how busy the Slasher had been. *The Sun*'s readers were told he had already made 10 attacks, while the *Sydney Morning Herald* headline said this was his 12th assault.

There was something else the press missed. Police had uncovered another clue from the Meyer house – a palmprint lifted from the windowsill in Rosalie's room. It was more evidence to add to the fingerprint from the Gurney house, but it didn't seem to be leading anywhere. Searches of fingerprint records weren't turning up any matches to the Gurney print. Police were wondering if, just maybe, the man they were chasing was a cleanskin who had never been in trouble with the law.

That would make their job a whole lot harder. As would news the following month that made Sydney readers wonder if any suburb in the city was safe from the Kingsgrove Slasher.

15

"All efforts by detectives and patrols of local residents have failed to catch him."
Sydney Morning Herald, December 15, 1956

The police – and the public – couldn't have known it at the time but there was something unusual about the Slasher's assaults on Valerie Thompson and Rosalie Meyer. They were committed in his usual stomping ground but he was no longer living nearby.

He was around 30 kilometres away, living in a guest house in Waiwera St, Lavender Bay, a trip that would have required crossing the Sydney Harbour Bridge. Yet in all the police questioning since made public, there is no indication that the new North Shore resident was ever asked why he continued to travel back over the bridge to the Slasher territory to commit crimes. Nor was he asked how he managed that feat, given it would seemingly require him to return to the boarding house room he and his wife called home before she woke.

A clue to how he did it may exist in the fact these two most recent crimes happened early on Monday mornings. His wife would tell the police in the early days of their marriage he would head home to visit his family in Kingsgrove. Perhaps he went over there on Sundays for the traditional Sunday roast and then chose to stay the night rather than travel back over the bridge. Maybe his wife came with him sometimes, maybe other times it was a trip he made alone.

Perhaps on October 28 and November 25 he headed to New England Drive alone. Then, after his father and new mother had gone to sleep, he could sneak out the back door to prowl the streets he knew well. And he could do it free from the chance of getting found out by a wife waking in the middle of the night to an empty space on his side of the bed.

By mid-December he'd grown confident enough to strike out closer to his new home north of the bridge. Surprisingly close in fact – just a 290-metre walk away. He just had to climb the stairs outside the boarding house up to the footpath, turn left along Waiwera Street and left into the downhill run of King George Street and follow it as it hooks right into Bay View Street and runs a block from the edge of Lavender Bay.

A 150-metre walk along Bay View Street would see him in front of a block of flats where 14-year-old Georgina Palmer lived. Her family's unit was at the rear, with a stretch of casement windows in Georgina's room offering a stunning view of the water and the Sydney Harbour Bridge. These days a home just a lazy stone's throw from the waters of the harbour comes with a steep price tag. But it wasn't always the case; through to the mid-1950s the area housed the working class employed in the ferries or boat-building trade, while those who could afford it headed to the bigger homes in the suburbs.

The Slasher was showing signs of being more confident in his ability to avoid capture. It was 3.30am; he'd worked out his wife was a heavy sleeper and unlikely to wake. But also, the McMahons Point area didn't offer the escape routes of bushland that had previously been a factor in choosing which homes would see him use the razor. A member of running and athletic clubs, as an adult, the Slasher was sure he could outrun the husband or father of any female he attacked.

But he wasn't stupid. He still went around to the back of the flats so he would be shielded from anyone passing by on the street. Georgina's neighbor had a ladder in their yard so the Slasher grabbed it to reach her windows, which were about two metres off the ground.

Georgina had left a towel hanging out of the window before she went to sleep at 9pm. The Slasher reached up for it, folded it and placed it on the window sill. Then he rested the upper edges of the ladder against the towel, to muffle any noise. Climbing several rungs, he looked in one of the open windows – Georgina had left them that way as it was a warm night. There the girl was, asleep in her bed directly under the window. He didn't even need to climb through the window; he just reached in with his razor and cut her left breast several times.

The Slasher may have had more planned for Georgina but she woke to see him standing at her window.

"Mummy, mummy! A man's in my room!"

At that he jumped down from the ladder and fled down Bay View Street. Her father darted out the door to see if he could spot the culprit but didn't see anything. Still in Georgina's room, her mother saw the small roses of blood soaking through into her pajama top; it was then they realised Georgina had been cut. The razor cuts weren't deep or long enough to require stitching but the memory of waking up and seeing a man at her window would linger in her mind for years to come.

Glen Humphries

The attack sent shudders through the city. That afternoon, *The Sun* hit the streets claiming it to be the work of the Kingsgrove Slasher. Not aware that he'd moved in just around the corner, it seemed to everyone as though he was widening his hunting ground. It was no longer the so-called "western suburbs" that lived in fear of forgetting to close a window or lock a door. That was a fact *The Sun* made sure it rammed home, waiting until the second paragraph to claim police feared the Slasher "may launch a reign of terror on the North Shore".

"As this type of sexual perversion or aberration was very rare, everything supported the theory that the madman was the Kingsgrove Slasher [police] added."

To continue the fevered pitch, *The Sun* ran the story on the front page with a deep-etched head-and-shoulders photo of Georgina Palmer taking up most of the space. Around the photo of the "pretty" 14-year-old roared the headlines "Slasher in weird attack", 'Maniac gashes girl (14)" and "She woke to find man in room".

The story said a doctor who saw Georgina's wounds suggested the Slasher had used "a weird double-pronged instrument" in the attack; an error likely based on the fact that Georgina's twin razor cuts were parallel to each other.

The Sydney Morning Herald put the Slasher's tally at 30 assaults – three times the actual number. In an exercise in stating the obvious, the *Herald* wrote, "Detectives believe the attacker is a sexual pervert of a type which gets satisfaction from slashing assaults."

In an odd footnote, a man pretending to be a policeman would knock on the Palmers' door the night after the attack. The man identified himself as a member of the vice squad and began questioning Georgina. Sensing something was not right, her mother called the squad and found the man was lying. The real police arrived and arrested 20-year-old Allan Theodore Bell from Caringbah.

In January Bell would appear before Magistrate AS Tunchon, where the man's solicitor told the court "Bell had been receiving psychiatric treatment from a Macquarie Street doctor and other doctors". The magistrate found that Bell's actions were "possibly nothing more than extreme foolishness" and recorded no conviction while placing the man on a £20 good behaviour bond.

16

"It's the first night I have gone to bed without keeping my hockey stick handy for protection."
Ruth Marks, *Daily Mirror*, December 28, 1956

Any confidence the Slasher gained by striking out in his new North Shore base was apparently short-lived. Just five days after leaning into Georgina Palmer's McMahons Point bedroom, he returned to the collection of suburbs he knew so well.

Having already prowled through houses in several of those suburbs, he added a new one to the list in Turrella. On the train line, it was three stops closer to the city than Kingsgrove and was not far from bushland that bordered Wolli Creek as it cut through the suburbs. Both the train station and the bush with its rough trails would become increasingly significant to the Slasher. And also to the man who would eventually capture him.

On December 19, less than a week before Christmas, 17-year-old Lorraine Cousins and her parents arrived home to Walker Street around 10.30pm after a family night out. As it was late, everyone said their good nights and retired to their bedrooms. Once inside hers Lorraine took her clothes off to dress for bed, leaving her slip on the carpeted floor near her bedroom window.

Her wet two-piece bikini was on her bed, so before she went to sleep, she picked it up, wrapped it in a towel so that it was not at all visible and placed it on the floor near the slip.

It was a warm December night and Lorraine opened the window slightly to let in some air. She then went to bed, finally falling asleep around 11pm. Not even the presence of the Slasher in her room that night would wake her up.

She rose at 7am and noticed her bedroom window was raised higher than she had left it the night before. She sat up in bed; that was when she noticed the flyscreen had been removed and discarded on the carpeted floor. Thinking it was strange and nothing more, Lorraine picked it up and put it back in place.

She headed out of her room and saw her mother in the kitchen and mentioned where she had found the screen. Her mother came with her back to her room, and then Lorraine realised the slip she had left on the floor was not there. Searching the room, she found it under her bedsheets.

Then the upper half of her swimsuit, which had been hidden from view inside the bundled-up towel, was lying at the top of the bed, near where she had been resting her head. And there were several razor cuts in it.

Her mother yelled to her husband to call the police.

When they arrived, the cuts in the slip were also spotted, as was a broken Gillette Blue razor stuck in the lining of her bikini top. Unlike almost all the other Slasher victims, Lorraine herself hadn't been cut at all. Which was fortunate – and strange. The Slasher seemed to have a need for the women and girls whose rooms he invaded to wake up and realise he was there. So much so that he viciously punched Lesley Coleman in the face when she wouldn't wake up. Yet he was in Lorraine's room totally undetected, where he likely could have done so much more than cut an item or two of clothing, he barely left a trace of his presence. He had even left untouched Lorraine's gold watch that was sitting in a recess in the bedhead. And he would later offer police no explanation for his actions.

The tale, a mundane one by Slasher standards, forced the media to beat it up. *The Sun* went with the screaming – and inaccurate – headline "Undies cut to pieces!". *The Mirror* saw fit to point out that Lorraine was "an attractive teenage girl". "It was an eerie feeling," she told the paper, "thinking that someone had been in the house while I slept, without us knowing it. There are some valuables around but the Slasher made no attempt to steal anything."

The December attacks on Palmer and Cousins would bring a rush of other "victims", certain they too had just had a run-in with the shadowy figure. On the night after the Slasher was at the Cousins' house in Turrella, Margaret Cahill insisted it was he who had climbed through her bedroom window in Mosman at 9.20pm. She claimed she was lying in bed with the light on listening to the radio when the man entered her room and attacked her.

There is much to suggest this was not the work of the Slasher. The time of 9.20pm was far too early to fit the Slasher MO. Also, Cahill claimed she was cut with a "sharp pronged instrument"; suspiciously, the very same weapon that media reports incorrectly claimed was used on Georgina Palmer. A doctor's examination found extensive cuts on her body; all superficial except for one that needed two stitches.

If that wasn't enough, her bedding, mattress and heavy curtains were also slashed, which suggested the "attacker" was in the room with her for quite some time – even after, as she claimed, she called out to her father for help as soon as he entered. A CIB detective would diplomatically tell *The Mirror* there was "no connection with the notorious Kingsgrove Slasher", leaving unsaid the high likelihood that the only slasher in Cahill's room was Cahill herself.

December also saw McMahons Point resident Muriel Harrison call the cops after she was up at 2am making a coffee and heard the front gate rattling. "I'd read the story about the Slasher being at McMahons Point," the 21-year-old told *The Mirror*. "I was scared and didn't want to take any risks so I rang the police." When the sun came up, she'd gone outside and found a drain cover outside the kitchen had been moved. "Someone standing outside the window could have done it," she said, sounding very much like someone trying to justify her rather large over-reaction.

Two days after Christmas 11-year-old Jill Howard said she heard footsteps outside her bedroom window at Daisy Avenue, Penshurst, when she was coming back from the toilet. "I was walking to my bed from the bathroom about 3am when I heard several heavy footsteps outside my window," she told *The Mirror*. "I was terrified. I jumped straight under my bed and lay there holding my breath. When the footsteps stopped I screamed for mum and dad."

The Sun insisted it was the Slasher, with Jill's father believing he had followed her eldest daughter home that night. That same *Sun* story reported that one Shirley Stevens said a man had reached into her bedroom window and touched her chest, a Miss Chard had awoken to find a man reaching in her window and pulling away her bedsheets and teen Jeanette Cooper had her dress slashed while on a crowded train at Parramatta.

A day later *The Sun* decided it was the Slasher who climbed into the bed of 16-year-old Ruth Marks of Yagoona. Under the utterly tabloid headline "Near-naked prowler", she told the paper she had been woken at around 4am by someone touching her arm. She opened her eyes and saw a bare-chested man bending over her. "He whispered to me – his voice was deep and horrible – 'It's alright, honey. Move over'." It had been the first night she'd gone to sleep without her hockey stick for protection - and also her last, she swore.

Amidst all the faux Slasher coverage, *The Sun* published an overview of the police hunt for the "mystery pervert".

"At intervals since July, this elusive maniac, whom police and psychiatrists classify as one of the most unusual types of perverts ever to operate in this state, has staged carefully-planned slashings. Each time he has disappeared without leaving a clue."

In a statement that surely wouldn't have comforted local residents, CIB boss Superintendent Calman effectively said the police didn't have the slightest idea of the Kingsgrove Slasher's identity. "Police have been unable to obtain anything but a flimsy description of practically no value," he said. "We must rely on public help to report anyone acting suspiciously at night or in the early morning hours."

It would be much the same story for another two and a half years.

17

"People often take their lives when they do not mean to, City Coroner JA Letts, SM, said today."
The Sun, March 28, 1957

For a serial criminal like the Slasher, he did something very strange in 1957. He stopped. For more than a year – 455 days in fact – he would give up the razor. It was a sizeable gap in the narrative, one that would confuse police when the Slasher returned and launched a spate of attacks in 1958 – though not as many as the 11 he had committed in 1956.

One police theory on his return was that he had been in a mental hospital or jail and had picked up where he left off upon release. It was a theory that would see CIB detectives trawling through prison and hospital records looking for anyone whose release coincided with the Slasher's return. While a reasonable theory, it was also a dead end as the Slasher hadn't spent a day in jail or a hospital up to that point.

Prior to his return in 1958 some investigators wondered if the solution to the Slasher case was found in a Bexley backyard in early 1957. A suburb just southeast of Kingsgrove, Bexley was close enough to many victims' homes to make it conceivable that the Slasher could have made his home there. And a discovery there on January 11 would, in hindsight, make some police wonder if it explained why the Slasher had been silent in 1957. On that January morning, Raymond Redfern, a hairdresser living in Carrington Street, Bexley, happened to look over the fence he shared with his neighbour, a city executive named William Tickle.

His neighbour was in the yard, but he was in no state to share any greetings. Tickle was dead, hanging from the clothesline with a length of rope around his neck. But this wasn't a suicide; as evidenced by what Tickle was wearing as he dangled from the clothesline – a bra, stockings and women's shoes. When police arrived on the scene, they would find a collection of women's clothing in his garage.

The 45-year-old Tickle was a bachelor. The death notice placed in the *Sydney Morning Herald* (which said he died "suddenly") lists no wife, just parents and a sister. He would be cremated just days after his death.

Due to the nature of Tickle's death, a coroner's investigation was carried out. City Coroner JA Letts found he had died from misadventure while engaged in autoeroticism, which would have been quite scandalous in the 1950s. "Often people do not mean to take their lives or they change their mind when it is too late," Letts said.

While there was no suggestion that Tickle was the Slasher at the time he was found hanging on the line, as time passed and there were no more assaults, some saw Tickle as a likely candidate. He lived by himself and so could come and go as he pleased, he appeared to be a "pervert" (as the Slasher was tagged) and his death occurred just weeks after the Cousins swimsuit slashing. So perhaps he was their man.

But he wasn't. The Slasher was alive and well throughout 1957; he was just trying to do the right thing by his wife. He would later tell police that she was the reason he left the razors in the bathroom alone for more than a year. "I tried to settle down for the wife's sake," he told Detective Doyle back at the police station after his capture.

Which seems like a strange statement from a man who got a thrill from going into women's bedroom to slash them. But there did seem to be genuine affection between the two. During their marriage, Jean – known to friends as Jenny – went away for a fortnight's holiday on her own. Rather than use his time alone to prowl the streets as much as he wanted without fear of being discovered by his partner, the Slasher travelled up to join his wife a few days later.

When the truth about their fellow tenant was revealed, people living at the boarding house in Waiwera Street, Lavender Bay, would talk about how the couple would hold hands as they headed off to the city for work, and would walk into the dining room of an evening hand in hand. "They had a great love for each other," one resident would tell *The Mirror* after the court had passed sentence on the Slasher in late 1959.

One of those tenants happened to be *Mirror* reporter Nancy Thom, who lived under the same roof as the Slasher and his wife Jean for six months without suspecting a thing. After he was sentenced, she was given half a page in the paper (complete with a byline – a rarity in those days) to talk about her amazement that the "personable, attractive" man she knew was the Slasher.

"He and his wife did not mix very much with the other guests," Thom wrote. "They were so obviously deeply in love that, for the majority of the time, they required only each other's company.

"I used to watch them, enviously, walk up the hill to the North Sydney station each morning on their way to work. They always walked arm in arm, and they chatted happily to each other all the way.

"To the outsider, they were a young couple completely wrapped up in each other."

While Jean was unaware of her husband's secret life, she may have had a skeleton of her own in the closet. Her father was an alleged child molester. After his wife Agnes died – possibly in childbirth – Ernest Henry Garland didn't appear to want to raise Jean and her two siblings and so they were put in homes. But he stayed in the Taree-Gloucester area of NSW.

In December 1935, six months after Agnes' death, Ernest was at his ferryman's job on the Manning River crossing, just south of Coopernook, where the Garland family once called home. That month he saved Allen Barrett, a small boy who had fallen into the waters of the Manning River.

Without bothering to stop the engine Ernest dove in the water fully clothed and managed to reach the boy. A man on the ferry threw out a lifebuoy to the pair while someone else stopped the ferry's engine.

"Others launched the boat attached to the ferry but this was in a leaky condition and by the time it was rowed to the valiantly struggling ferryman and child they were halfway to Croki [a town downriver] owning to the swiftness of the current," the *Manning River Times* reported.

"By the time they reached the shore the boat was half-full of water. Mr Garland had swallowed a large quantity of water and he was almost exhausted."

The following year Ernest would be awarded a medal for bravery for his actions.

Night Terrors

Ten years later, Ernest would try something similar, only this time he would sink beneath the waters and never be seen alive again. He was a few hundred kilometres west of Taree, on the shore of the Barrington River in flood. Spying some cattle on an island in the middle of the river, he decided to enter the waters and bring them to higher ground. Ignoring the protests of two men he was with, Ernest stripped and waded into the cold waters of the Barrington.

The two men, who would give evidence at the coroner's inquest, would say he swam downstream for a short while before apparently realising he'd made a dangerous mistake. Ernest turned to face them and raised his hand in the air, signalling for help. It was then that the current took him towards a fallen oak tree, where he hit his head and disappeared under the water.

His presumed drowning meant a court case would have to be put on hold. On March 23, 1945, at Gloucester – not far from the waters that would claim him – Ernest was alleged to have assaulted two 11-year-old girls and had "committed an act of indecency" on both of them. The newspapers of the area noted no further details of the offences, though the language clearly points to some sort of sexual assault.

While Ernest had been charged over the offences, he was still a free man. The trial had been stood over several times and had yet to begin three months later when he waded into the Barrington River. His disappearance after hitting the oak tree meant the case would be stood over again.

It wasn't a case of Ernest looking to fake his death so as to disappear; in January 1946 a body would be found hanging from a ti-tree in the Barrington, almost two kilometres downriver from where he had last been seen. The corpse was nothing but bones and body tissue; there were no teeth in its head and the right hand and foot were missing, as was the left leg below the knee.

Still, the circumstantial evidence was strong that it was Ernest. His cousin Sidney, a dairy farmer in the area, was able to identify the skeleton as Ernest. The dead man had a "peculiar shaped head and stooped shoulders" and Sid could see these features in the skeleton fished out of the river. That was enough for the coroner, who ruled it was the body of Ernest Leslie Garland.

It was a ruling that meant there would be no justice for two 11-year-old girls in Gloucester. While Jean was estranged from her father, it's highly probable she knew about the charges against him as she lived in the area until 1954, which is when she met her husband. Until the court papers are discovered, the identities of those two 11-year-old girls will remain unknown. But Jean was born in 1934, which would have made her 11 years old in March 1945, when Ernest committed those sexual assaults.

Maybe she was hiding not one secret, but two.

18

"I didn't use anything to hit her with, I am sure. I just punched her on the head and face."
The Kingsgrove Slasher's police interview, May 1, 1959

It's clear that the Slasher was a morning person. An *early* morning person. His preference was to stalk the streets until something told him he had the right house. Whatever process he used to determine which home to hit, it never occurred before midnight. The first attack, against Margaret Campbell as she made out with a boyfriend in his car, happened at 9.30pm. Though that was a crime of opportunity; he was out doing the rounds of a peeping Tom and came across the couple in the car and took a chance.

All the others happened when his female victims were at home asleep; where he knew they'd be for hours and so there was no rush to find the perfect place for that night's raid. For him it seemed to be as much about the journey as the destination.

And so it wasn't until 12.40am that he woke up seven-year-old Anne Willis by tugging at her pyjamas; the hands on the clock had passed 3am before he entered Rosalie Meyer's room and smashed her head with a lump of wood, and he was happy to prowl until 4am when he let himself in via an unlocked door and punched Lesley Coleman into unconsciousness.

And prowl he did; the Coleman assault was one of five that would occur after 4am but that didn't mean the Slasher had been tucked snuggly in bed before getting up in the early hours to attack a woman in her bed. By the time he found himself in Coleman's bedroom or Judith Gurney's (4.30am) or Gloria Geyson's at 5am, he'd been in any number of other people's homes that night. The Slasher mightn't have chosen to leave his mark to let the sleeping household know he'd been inside their home, but he'd been there. Because he liked doing it – and while he would tell police there weren't many nights when he stayed out for a long time, his record of crimes suggested otherwise.

At the Slasher trial, Detective Sergeant Doyle told the court of the accused's habit of prowling for hours while suburbia slept. "On some occasions he may have prowled around for hours and hours before he eventually stopped at a suitable place," Doyle said. "One night he prowled from about 9pm until 5.15am."

While he didn't name the victim the Slasher found that night, it was likely Geyson - the one committed closest to the light of the morning. Another of those attacks after 4am was one on a 13-year-old girl named Robin Lesley Williams. Living in the North Shore suburb of Greenwich, she was a half-hour walk northwest from the Slasher's Waiwera Street digs. And she was the Slasher's first victim in 455 days. There is nothing in the evidence handed to the court during either the committal hearing or the trial to explain why he lost his self-control and returned to the dark streets. Was he succumbing to a long-running urge inside of him, or was it a desire that came all of a sudden? Or had he been out at other times during that 455-day period and no one connected those crimes to him?

The latter is certainly plausible, given that the newspapers didn't link the Williams attack to him either. The tabloids didn't appear to run a single news story of the attack; which is odd when you consider their interest in the case in 1957 and the almost obsessive coverage his exploits would get from late 1959 through to his capture and trial. In fact, it seems the journos on the Slasher beat didn't add Williams to the list of crimes until the cops figured it out months after the Slasher found himself outside the girl's Greendale Street house in the early hours of March 18, 1958.

People had forgotten about the Slasher; their fear of who might come through an unlocked door or open window had left them. This is perhaps why schoolgirl Williams left her bedroom window open as far as it would go and the blind up when she went to sleep around 9pm. Even though her room was located around the side of a house backing onto bushland. And her bedroom window was less than a metre off the ground; easy for someone to climb through.

As it was, the Slasher chose not to climb into the room. He didn't have to; her bed was right underneath the low window. He could reach in for her while leaving his feet planted outside. Which is just what he did.

While he was carrying a razor with him, he'd found one on Williams' windowsill and used that to slash her bedsheets. While the schoolgirl was still sleeping, he lent in and groped the 13-year-old's breasts hard enough to leave bruising and then punched her in the face several times. That roused her and she woke to feel his hands wrapping around her neck and beginning to squeeze. He would never offer an explanation as to whether he was trying to choke the girl, but there doesn't seem to be any other reason to grab someone around the throat.

Williams was able to scream out for her parents, which stopped the Slasher's onslaught and he fled before mum and dad made it to her bedroom. Turning on the light, her mother noticed the slashes in the blanket and the marks on her face and neck. Surprisingly, Williams seems to have gone back to sleep in her bed after the attack; she would later tell the magistrate at the committal hearing that she woke up again after 7am and noticed the soreness and bruising on her chest.

By then the Slasher had made it back home, where he would remain quiet for another eight months before moving house. That move would put him in Arncliffe, on the eastern edge of Slasher territory – just a kilometre from the home of victim Lorraine Cousins. The return to familiar ground where he felt more comfortable, more easily able to spend hours at night away from his wife without raising her suspicions was the trigger for a series of six attacks over a three-month period.

They would see a return of the fear those suburbs hadn't felt since 1956 and would usher in relentless media coverage of the Slasher. That coverage would further stoke those suburban fears but also make the job of the soon-to-be-established Slasher Patrol much harder. And it would also make things hard for the Slasher – the man who said he loved to be chased would come to rue the sudden increase in tabloid attention he was about to get.

19

"Woman slashed as she slept"
The Sun, November 19, 1958

Two years after their marriage – in September 1958 – Jean and her husband left the Lavender Bay guest house and moved to a small home in Park St, Arncliffe. Since they'd walked down the aisle, he'd invaded five women's bedrooms and slashed their clothes, their bedding, punched some in the face or hit them with a block of wood. He would commit six more while living in Arncliffe yet Jean seemed to have no idea.

It's hard to believe; she slept next to him but never noticed his side of the bed was empty, never was roused by him climbing into bed in the dead of night. She would even ask him to install locks on the windows in their Park St home, unaware the Slasher was already inside. She wouldn't find out who she'd been married to until the night of his capture, when Detective Sgt Doyle brought him to her doorstep. He'd asked Doyle if he could tell her himself, rather than have her find out the truth from the tabloid papers that afternoon.

If she didn't know, it was partially because she was a heavy sleeper, and also because her husband went to some lengths to cover his tracks. Sometimes he would plan ahead, telling her in the morning that he had to work back that night. She would go to bed early and, being a heavy sleeper, wouldn't notice what time he arrived home from "work". So she wouldn't wonder why the amount in his pay packet was still the same despite working overtime, he would throw in some extra cash to make it all seem above board.

Other times, when he was home of an evening, he would wait until she was getting ready for bed and tell her he was going on a training run. "I would put on my old sweater, a pair of trousers and rubber boots and off I would go," he told police. "She would be sound asleep when I got home and she wouldn't know whether it was 11, 12 or three o'clock in the morning."

The Slasher waited for a month to pass in his new digs at Arncliffe before deciding to head out for a "training run". He'd end up staying close to home, venturing less than a kilometre away to Walker Street, Turrella, the same street where he stood in the bedroom of sleeping teen Lorraine Cousins and cut up her swimsuit. At 3am on November 19 – a Wednesday – he found himself outside a house just a few doors down from the Cousins', where Valma Rogers lived with her husband Richard. He was about to slice someone open.

It wasn't Valma or Richard who would suffer this, but Valma's mother Marguerite Austin. The 64-year-old woman was confined to bed on doctor's orders, suffering a kidney inflammation known as nephritis. Rather than have the divorcee stay alone in her own house at nearby Hannam Street – a two-minute drive away – her daughter brought her into the spare bedroom in her home. A decision that would end up being a case of "wrong place, wrong time".

Night Terrors

At around 8.30pm, Mrs Austin had gone to bed in a room located on the side of the house with casement windows overlooking the driveway. Her doctor had prescribed sleeping tablets to help her get some rest and she'd taken one that night, leaving a casement window above her bed open to let in a breeze. Later, about 1am, Valda would bring her mother a drink of water, having woken to give her own daughter some medication. Then she turned off the kitchen light and went back to her own bedroom at the front of the house.

When the Slasher arrived at the Rogers' Walker Street home, he found the open window at the side of the house quite inviting. But it was set too high up the wall for him to reach in, so he crept into the backyard to look for something to stand on. He found a wooden fruit box near a backyard fern house that would do the trick, and so he carried it around to the open window. Placing it on the ground, he stepped up and looked through the window and spied the sleeping form of Mrs Austin on the bed directly below him.

He must have lent in through the window and started pawing at Mrs Austin's bedding, for she would later tell the court she remembered the feeling of the blankets slipping off. She pulled them back up and rolled over onto her left side, facing the window, and went back to sleep.

Perhaps the one open window the Slasher lent into wasn't close enough for him to reach his victim. So he reached around to the next window in the row and quietly opened it. Next he stepped down from the wooden fruit box, moved it about a metre so it was under the second window and climbed back on it.

What he would do next would shock himself when he read it in the afternoon newspapers while sitting at home with his wife. Taking a razor, he cut through a couple of blankets, a bed sheet and the two pairs of men's flannelette pajamas Mrs Austin was wearing.

It wasn't a neat single slash that cut through all that bedding; he admitted he had to go back and forth in a sawing motion to get through it all. And in that sawing motion he cut deeply into Mrs Austin herself, leaving a massive 12-centimetre gash along the right side of her abdomen.

Mrs Austin woke, feeling a sense of struggling against something. "I jumped out of bed," she would tell a journo from *The Sun*, "turned on the light and found myself covered in blood. I started to feel weak and called my daughter." She would later make a point of telling a courtroom it wasn't a scream, saying she wasn't "the screaming kind". When her daughter came in, Mrs Austin was standing in a pool of her own blood from the wound to the abdomen. "I was so stunned I could hardly move," Valma told *The Sun*. "There was blood everywhere and mum's bedclothes were ripped to shreds."

The police and ambulance were called and, as part of their investigations, Mrs Austin's blood-soaked pajamas were taken as evidence. The ambulance took Mrs Austin and her daughter to St George Hospital, where she was seen by Dr Michael Harpur. He had to place one long internal running stitch to close the gaping wound before then completely closing it up with 12 more stitches. Then the doctor administered a tetanus shot and gave her some morphine for the pain. While Dr Harpur would not be asked in court whether the wound was life-threatening, newspaper reports on the day of the attack would claim "doctors said had the wound been a fraction deeper, she might have died".

Despite the fact his last known attack – at the time – was nearly two years ago, the afternoon papers were quick to name the Slasher as the culprit. *The Sun* played down the connection; while using the word "slashed" in the headline, a subhead explained it was an "attack by prowler". It wasn't until the fourth paragraph that the Kingsgrove Slasher was mentioned.

The Mirror wasn't interested in burying the lead. "Maniac Slasher returns" read the headline and the first paragraph said detectives feared it was the work of the "crazed Kingsgrove Slasher". On the evening of November 19, the Slasher himself would read those newspaper stories at home. He wasn't thrilled about the coverage – for a man who said he slashed bedding because he wanted his victims to know he'd been in their room, he had a dislike of newspapers reporting that message more widely. Said it made it harder for him to do his thing.

What drew his attention was the extent of Mrs Austin's injuries. In a statement that's hard to read in anything but a self-absorbed tone, one of a person more interested in his own feelings rather than anyone else's, he would tell police, "... I must admit that when I read of what I had done to old Mrs Austin it jolted me and made me think a bit." But it obviously didn't jolt him so much that it made him stop what he was doing. In a perverse attempt at mitigation he would tell Detective Doyle he was trying to cut her breast at the time – "I thought I was cutting her higher up," he said.

As would soon become commonplace, the following day's tabloids featured stories about other prowlers and "perverts" with hints that this too could be the work of the Slasher. One of those happened to 19-year-old Joy Dostine at Kogarah. Just after midnight on November 20, the teen was walking home to Beverly Hills when she noticed a car had been following her. She broke into a run, the car speeding ahead and cutting her off. Then a man jumped from the driver's seat – and Dostine insisted he was stark naked. "Shut up or you really will get hurt," he apparently told her. She started to run and the man, despite being naked and having a car at his disposal,

81

ran after her on foot. When lights came on in several homes nearby, he returned to his car and drove off.

"Police are probing a theory that the pervert may have been the same man responsible for the slashing of a 64-year-old woman yesterday morning at Turrella," *The Sun* said. It's a pretty safe bet police weren't doing that at all, given it in no way matches the Slasher's well-established pattern. Aside from that, the story of a man driving naked through the streets of Kogarah just doesn't have the ring of truth about it.

The Mirror followed suit under the headline "Prowlers terrorise women", though the incidents the paper cited fell a long way short of anyone being terrorised. A nurse saw a tall man "prowling" the grounds of a convalescent home at Ashfield. A pair of men were spotted in the grounds of a girls' school, St Scholastica's College in Glebe. Curiously the journalist saw fit to note that "one left a coat hanging on a tree" when they "escaped". The third was the naked man reported by the 19-year-old Dostine.

The press went for it again a day later, reporting on a Paddington prowler. Betty Leary and her mother and four children were all in the same bedroom after 11pm when Leary claimed she heard footsteps on the verandah outside. When a man's face appeared at the bedroom window, she flung a shoe at him, shattering the glass. "He ran away," Leary concluded. There was no explanation as to why six people were all sleeping in the same bedroom.

20

"The crazed Kingsgrove Slasher, who terrified three young women early today in lightning visits, has police baffled."
Daily Mirror, December 4, 1958

Razor blades now are a little different to what was used for shaving in the 1950s. Today the razors are contained within a disposable head; the whole thing is thrown away when the blades themselves become dull and a new head is added. In the 1950s it was just the blade itself that was replaced; the head – which was attached to the handle – opened up and a new rectangular razor blade was slid into place.

It was those rectangular blades the Slasher would use, though not on himself; he was an electric razor man all the way. When it came to arming himself for night-time jaunts, he would usually use his wife's Gillette Gem blades that she used for shaving under her arms, as he told police. Occasionally he would splurge on a pack of Gillette Blue blades, likely having to hide them from his wife lest she ask why a man with an electric razor needed blades.

Unlike a straight razor (also known as a cut-throat razor) there was no handle for the Slasher to hold while cutting his victims. He was able to avoid cutting himself while holding the razor because he only used single-edge blades; though of course the fact his victims were usually fast asleep when he attacked also helped.

Whether the blades came from his own stash or his wife's, the Slasher never kept them as a souvenir; once he had used them on a victim, he threw them away. There were only two instances where he didn't use a razor blade, and one of them occurred in a home in Jacobson Avenue, Kyeemagh, a block back from Botany Bay, where the airport is now visible from the end of the street. And he accidentally left behind his weapon of choice as a clue for police.

The Slasher had to travel some distance to get to the bedroom of the teenaged Elaine Kelly, which was a four-kilometre walk - and he insisted he always prowled on foot, never using a vehicle. He did cut the distance down somewhat by taking a short cut along a sewer pipe, but it was still the furthest he'd travelled on foot from his home. And to complicate matters, he did it in driving rain.

In an indication of how powerful the Slasher's urges were, a night spent walking around in the rain didn't deter him. Despite the official start of summer three days earlier, the city copped a drenching. By 3pm on Tuesday, December 3, there were 84 millimetres in the rain gauges, and it kept falling long into the night as well. Yet he headed out into the storm, walking in the rain for kilometres before he would have arrived at Jacobson Avenue, cold and very, very wet.

Despite the torrential rain falling from the skies, the Slasher did not appear to be in any great hurry to find a victim and return home. He made his way through several backyards in the street; he found a bra hanging from a clothesline and chose to take it for his own pleasure. By about 4am – with the sunrise expected less than a half-hour later, he walked down the side of Kelly's house. Despite the awful weather the teen – who had left school and was working as a secretary – had left two casement windows open to the night air and the noise of the rain. So the Slasher, dripping wet, reached in to remove the flyscreens covering the openings and climbed inside.

He crept over to her bed and crouched alongside it so, should Kelly wake she wouldn't see him. The teen was disturbed by the feeling of her blankets being pulled off her; as she woke from sleep Kelly also realised she could hear someone breathing heavily. Petrified, she lay very still in her bed for a while, before realising someone was on the floor next to her bed. That was when she found her voice and screamed, forcing the Slasher to flee from her bedside and dive out the window. "I could hear him breathing heavily," she would tell police. "Then I screamed and screamed until mum and dad rushed in."

Getting out of bed, she found a sopping wet bra on the floor of her bedroom; the Slasher's souvenir had fallen out of his pocket when he fled. Despite the night-time shock, Kelly still went to work that morning – she hadn't been physically harmed. It wasn't until she returned home that she noticed her blanket had been cut; the Slasher had done that as he pulled it from her body. Police took the blanket as evidence, and found the cutting implement – a medical scalpel – had been caught up in it. The Slasher had taken it from his warehouse job, where they stocked them among a range of other items.

Police had collected the razor blades he had left at the scene of earlier attacks but they were mass-produced items, easily purchased at any market or chemist. They carried no potential to unlock the case. They may have had fingerprints on them but police had already collected different parts of his finger and handprints at the scenes of earlier crimes, and they hadn't helped them to home in on a suspect. His prints weren't on record with the police – he'd committed no previous crimes – so any prints were only of use to identify or eliminate a suspect they had in custody. They'd be no help in finding that suspect. But a medical scalpel, well that was a different story – the police looked at that as a real clue.

Since the Slasher's return in November, the police had taken the investigation more seriously than before, where for so many months it was handled by the local detectives. Now, the head of the CIB Superintendent Calman appointed one of his own detectives to lead the investigation.

The man who got the gig actually lived in Kingsgrove, just a 20-minute walk away from the house the Slasher grew up in. Detective Sergeant Brian Doyle had already gained a reputation as a cleanskin, as an honest cop. It was a reputation that didn't sit well with some of the bent cops in the force; one of whom was also a CIB detective. Ray Kelly was a cop with a lot of connections and informants in the Sydney underworld and soon enough he got his hands dirty.

In his book *Can of Worms* journalist Evan Whitton said Kelly would favour certain informants by overlooking their crimes, set up underworld killings under the guise of police actions, was involved in abortion rackets and was infamous for offering false testimony (verballing) in order to see a suspect jailed. He became so well-known for it that he earned the nickname "Verbal".

He would be one of the detectives charged with interviewing young officers keen to enter plainclothes work. As part of the interview process, he would ask the officer if they were prepared to fit up a criminal if necessary. If the answer was yes, then they got the thumbs up. If it was a no, he'd say "Give him back to the Cardinal, he's no good to me". The Cardinal was Kelly's derogatory nickname for Doyle – reflecting his Catholic religion and also his scrupulously honest nature.

One of Doyle's last cases before heading up the Slasher unit involved an accusation of a sergeant accepting a bribe. In September

1958, Stephen Roylett's wife and two children went on holiday. While they were away, Roylett "got mixed up with a married woman", Sgt Doyle would tell the court. They had a few drinks and then the pair jumped in Roylett's car and headed to his house. On the way, Roylett drove off the road and mounted the footpath.

The woman would be taken to hospital suffering a fractured nose and shock. Doyle became involved when Roylett complained to police the woman was trying to blackmail him, demanding £100 or she'd tell his wife. During that investigation he revealed to Doyle he had offered Sgt Lionel Lorenz a bribe on the day of the accident as a way to keep it all from his wife.

"This defendant suggested to the sergeant that he pay him £25 to let the whole matter drop," Sgt Doyle told the court.

"After some discussion, the defendant says, it was agreed and the money was paid by him to the sergeant at Lidcombe police station on September 2. The defendant very fairly admits that no approach was made to him by the sergeant, but that, on the contrary, the defendant himself was the initial mover."

Roylett's lapse of judgement would be forgiven by his wife but not by the court, which fined him £15. In a separate trial Sgt Lorenz – likely charged by Doyle as the investigating detective – would plead not guilty. Lorenz's lawyer would claim Roylett was a liar, and that the sergeant was not at the station at 5pm when the bribe was handed over. The court would find Lorenz not guilty of accepting a bribe that another court found Roylett guilty of handing over.

The case served as a reflection of Doyle's character; rather than turn a blind eye to the allegations of police bribery, he investigated the case and saw a sergeant have to stand up in court to answer to the allegations. In a force at the time where bribes large or small wouldn't have been unusual, where some may have even considered it a perk of the job, Doyle had firmly drawn his line in the sand. It would take a man of strong character to turn up for work, knowing those on the other side of that line likely disliked him and didn't trust him.

Under the Doyle regime, Slasher squad detectives began with the theory that the answer to the Slasher's identity lay in the almost two-year break from December 1956 to November 1958 (they had yet to connect him to the apparent strangulation attempt on Robin Williams in March 1958). They figured a creature like the Slasher wouldn't, *couldn't*, just stop of his own accord so they began checking the jails and mental hospitals for male inmates whose time inside matched those dates. With no description, no match for the fingerprints and no other crims who seemed willing to dob him in (because he didn't move in those circles to begin with), it was pretty much all they had.

The situation was so dire that Calman, the CIB boss, issued a public plea that surely someone out there had to know something. "Somebody must know that this person has this kink and must know that this person goes out at odd hours and has peculiar habits," he said.

"We appeal to these people to come forward in the interests of the community and in the interests of the poor unfortunate person himself. This type of person is to be pitied and obviously needs medical treatment."

Prisons department psychiatrist Dr John McGeorge weighed in with some helpful advice for young women in the Slasher zones, which included them not leaving a light on after going to sleep. An odd piece of advice given all the Slasher's victims had been asleep in dark rooms.

He also gave his expert opinion on the Slasher's motivation, which would end up rather wide of the mark; "His perversion is probably caused by a strong hatred of the female sex. I am sure he could not conceal his mentally unbalanced state from, say, a close relative or friend or the people he lives with."

21

"Police ask 'do you know the Slasher?'."
Sydney Morning Herald, December 5, 1958

The Slasher's visit to Elaine Kelly at Jacobson Avenue put the wind up the residents of Kyeemagh. Joe Douse lived in the same street and he told the *Herald* that his daughter Margaret went to visit a friend the night before who lived just 50 metres away; and she took a 17cm-long knife for protection.

"I'll use the knife too if anyone attacks me," the teen said. "Last week when I went out I carried a hammer."

In response to the attack on Kelly a committee of men decided to form a vigilante group. The patrols, which would occur on foot and in cars, were the brainchild of Rockdale Council alderman Keith Hislop.

"The Slasher has every woman in the area terrified," he said. "Every house has its windows and doors locked at night. Women, if they go out at night are arming themselves with knives and hammers."

Alderman Hislop said the patrols will not carry weapons and will call police if they spotted a suspicious person. Still, the patrols had a whiff of Dad's army about them — they would only patrol streets where a few residents had the phone connected in case the police needed to be called.

The hysteria swept one suburb to the east, across the simply-named Muddy Creek to Banksia. Parts of the suburb still look the way it would have back in the Slasher's day with many of the homes still sporting the postwar dark-brick-and-red-roof style popular at the time. It was in Tabrett Street, which runs to the west until the Princes Highway gets in the way, that the fear of the Slasher led to scores of people flooding the streets in December 1958, looking to hunt down the phantom.

It started at midnight on December 7 when Noel McKinnon's wife woke him up after hearing a noise in the house. He walked out into the hall and spotted a man standing outside the bedroom door of his six-year-old daughter Lynette. Despite saying it was pitch black in the house, he managed to see what the man was wearing — white shirt with the sleeves rolled up, dark trousers, sandshoes.

McKinnon rushed at the intruder and started grappling with him. The man made "guttural noises" and bared his teeth at the homeowner before growling at him like a wild dog.

"It was an eerie experience," he told the *Herald*. "I kept on punching. My main fear was that he had a knife." The man broke free of the clinch and ran off, crashing through the screen door at the front of the house; McKinnon had left the door open because it was a hot night.

"I chased him to the gate and, as he was about to vault over it, I hit him with a rabbit punch on the back of the neck." The punch seemed to disorientate the man and he fell to the footpath. But then he got up and ran off like a deer.

"I'm a pretty good runner myself but he left me standing. I chased him for a quarter of a mile but I wasn't in the race."

A number of police cars had turned up by the time he returned home, as well as several newspaper prowl cars with police radios inside. A search of the streets began, with reporters, photographers and neighbours milling about outside in the middle of the night.

The police were back at Banksia the following night after a call from a taxi driver. He'd dropped off a "suspicious" man outside a house, but when police checked, the man did not live there. A search revealed no sign of him.

December 10 and the cars were rushing to Tabrett Street again after Mrs Appleby said she saw a man's hand reach through a window towards her sleeping two-year-old daughter Deborah.

"I heard my daughter cry and went into her bedroom," she said. "I saw the flyscreen ripped back and a man's hand waving through the window."

She shouted to her husband, parked in the lounge room watching the telly. He ran out the back door in time to see the man jumping their fence.

As well as police cars, 30 radio taxis arrived to help in the search. The Police Rescue truck was called in, so searchers could use spotlights mounted on the back. And of course, the journo prowl cars were there too.

Sgt Doyle was at the scene and would marvel at the sight of thousands of people on the streets of Banksia that night. He would later write about that night in a police report.

"On one night I witnessed a spectacle of about 2000 men, women and children scantily clad in night attire, lining the streets in the vicinity of Tabrett Street, Banksia, when an alarm had been raised that the notorious offender had been disturbed in the street (it was a bogus call)," he wrote.

"Many of the men seen that night, including boys 12 and 14 years of age, started a stampede around the district with rifles, going through the parks, canals etc in numbers, searching or pretending to search for some ghostlike figure of whom they knew nothing."

Doyle said he and other detectives had to step in to stop the residents' "wild west" tactics. One of those residents, 15-year-old Ian Hobson, would happily pose for *The Sun* photographer armed with his rifle. There he is, bolt-action rifle in one hand and torch in the other (despite the fact the photo is taken in daylight), peering over the neighbour's fence as if looking for the Slasher.

He claimed to be part of that mob the night before and pledged to shoot the Slasher if he ever returned to these here parts.

Mrs Appleby would make the front page of the following day's *Daily Mirror*, a photo of her pointing a torch at the footprints the intruder left in her backyard under thick black text that screamed "The Slasher strikes again!". She wasn't alone on that front page; she had to share it with a nightgown-clad Jean Morgan. In her right hand, she holds a pillow case with a large clean cut through it.

She would claim it was the Slasher's work. Just after 4am, she said, the Slasher crept into the bedroom where the 44-year-old was sleeping with her invalid husband and cut into her pillow, bedsheets and nightwear. Incredibly, despite this flurry of slashing, she was completely unscathed. The Slasher had even managed to cut through her bra without so much as nicking her skin.

"For a moment I could not move – I just stared at him," she told the press of the alleged attack. "He did not speak but turned quickly and leapt through the window." For someone who had just woken up in a dark room to find a man next to her bed, she supplied police with an astonishingly vivid description – black shirt and trousers, wearing a white peaked cap, rubber gloves and sandshoes.

When police arrived, they soon managed to round up a man wearing similar clothing and brought him back to the Morgan home in Bexley. Perhaps not expecting police to find someone who actually matched her description of what was likely an imaginary attacker, she said they'd got the wrong guy.

The papers didn't care, they'd worked out the Slasher sold papers. So they didn't need to wait for the police to say it was the Slasher's handiwork. Any prowler – whether real or imagined – was the Slasher and they would say so. In a bold headline on page one if they could. Hell, even someone saying they heard a noise outside that *might* have been made by a person (or a cat. Or a dog. Or even the wind) was the Slasher creeping about. And that's no exaggeration; under a front page head of "Terror! Face to face with Slasher" the *Mirror* told of a series of five "Slasher prowlings" the night before, which included a Mrs Tucker's report of hearing "a noise outside" while she was watching television.

December 1958 would prove to be a big month for Slasher coverage. Between the *Sydney Morning Herald* and the afternoon tabloid trio of the *Sun*, *Mirror* and *Telegraph*, a story on the Slasher ran almost every day. Competition was particularly fierce among the tabloids, with journos on the crime round always wary of being scooped by a rival. *The Mirror*'s Bill Jenkings would ring the home phone of his opposite number before going to bed; his reasoning was, if the other reporter picked up the phone at home Jenkings would know he wasn't out working on a story.

Few things were off limits in pursuit of a scoop; in his ghostwritten autobiography, Jenkings mentioned walking through the ashes of a home where a man has lost his life. Kicking over some burnt timber, he found a framed photo of the family. He picked it up and took it away, ignoring the protestations of police at the scene. It appeared in the paper the next day. Another *Mirror* journalist Steve

Dunleavy had to worry about his father, a photographer at *The Sun*. At a job in the Blue Mountains he stuck a shiv into the tyres of his dad's car to stop him from getting back to Sydney with a scoop.

Dad would get his revenge on the son during the Slasher's reign. One night both Dunleavys were on the Slasher beat when police believed they had cornered the spectre. Steve went into a laundry at the back of one of the houses where he reckoned the Slasher was hiding. His dad followed him. And locked the son inside – for hours.

The attention the press gave the Slasher wasn't welcomed by the lead detective. Doyle found the media's obsessive interest to be a hindrance to the investigation, believing they got in the way and also stirred up suburbia. "Journalists and photographers in numbers of radio-equipped cars patrolled the area nightly and kept continually tuned to VKG, listening to every message we got, both genuine and bogus," he wrote in one of his reports.

"They whipped up a state of near mass hysteria by the publication of concocted or exaggerated reports and photographs of his crimes in such a manner as to convey the impression to gullible readers that he was a phantom-like and maniacal will-o-the wisp."

As well as encouraging "neurotic women all over Sydney [to] claim that the Slasher had attacked them" the coverage also led to kooks ringing up saying they knew the Slasher or that they *were* the Slasher. *The Mirror* got one of the former when a man rang offering a deal. "The Slasher is a friend of mine and in need of help. If I tell you his name, will *The Mirror* hire a barrister to defend him in court? The Slasher is harmless but he badly needs the aid of a psychiatrist."

Needless to say the paper didn't pay for a barrister. But they did write a story about the phone call. Other pranksters would ring private homes, say they were the Slasher and that they were coming over tonight. Residents who got those calls would report them to police, even though it was obviously *not* the Slasher. Fourteen-year-old Noelene Batley was walking home in her suburb east of the airport when a car pulled up alongside her. Described as a mid-30s man with bushy eyebrows and wearing a "grubby-looking" T-shirt, the driver asked her if she knew about the Slasher. When she said yes, he replied "Well I'm it and I'll be round your district tonight." She ran home and her parents called the police, even though he was *obviously* not the Slasher either.

The Mirror would even get a letter from someone with too much time on their hands claiming to be the Slasher. Posted in Sydney but curiously bearing no stamps it was headed "WARNING" in block letters.

"You will never get me," the handwritten letter boasted, "not the cops or anybody. It is good to see myself in the paper.

"Slasher strikes again. Slasher again and all the time talk no action [sic]. I been in a search party myself. They are a lot of fools.

"But don't worry I will not harm anybody unless I am cornered and then kill or be killed.

"Once again I warn everybody stay out of my way or get hurt. Don't be a fool. Rather a living coward than a dead hero."

It was signed "The Slasher" and there was one more warning at the bottom of the page. "KEEP AWAY. I only warn people once. PS I just wrote a letter to the cops!".

It was handed over to CIB detectives for investigation, but of course it was a fake.

22

"My husband has got an iron bar handy too. If he ever has to use it, he'll kill this man."
Walker St resident Mrs R Ambler, *The Sun*, December 9, 1958

The fake letter and phone calls all came in the charged month of December 1958, when the Slasher was the top of list for the afternoon papers – and therefore the public as well. He was very much grist for the tabloid mill in Sydney of the late 1950s. *The Sydney Morning Herald* library holds a very thick file on the Slasher, bulging with clippings from the *Herald* and the three afternoon newspapers.

The December 1958 stories alone form a thick bundle, with even minor stories linked to the Slasher, if only to say police didn't believe this was his work. Here's a selection of those stories from the last month of 1958.

December 6 (*The Sun*): A prowler opens the bedroom window of Esmay Johnson's Stanmore home and shines a torch inside. "Miss Johnson challenged the man and he ran off".

December 8 (*The Mirror*): "Last night Miss Margaret Kobcroft (25), Illawarra St, Allawah, heard strange noises outside her bedroom window shortly before midnight.

"She lay silently in bed with the light on for more than 20 minutes listening to the muffled noises."

December 9 (*The Mirror*): "Council last night decided to clear a large area of lantana and tangled undergrowth at Carss Park Reserve at Blakehurst. Police believe the Slasher may use such areas as hideouts."

December 10 (*The Herald*): A student at a St George Girls High School dance carries a pair of flat-heeled shoes under her arm. They're so she can "run away from the Kingsgrove Slasher if he chases me home".

December 12 (*The Herald*): "About 9.30pm three police cars went to a house in St Elmo Parade, Kingsgrove, where a woman said a man had tapped on her window."

December 15 (*The Mirror*): A woman at Ramsgate reports hearing "strange noises" outside her house. The police find no trace of a prowler.

December 17 (*The Herald*): "Police searched in two suburbs in the St George area last night after women reported that they heard someone tapping on doors and windows."

December 19 (*The Mirror*): Three police cars rush to an Elizabeth Bay convent after a nun says she saw the shape of a man through a frosted glass window.

December 23 (*The Sun*): Police in the St George area respond to four cases of "frightened women" reporting tapping on their windows. "Later the women said the wind could have caused their windows to rattle".

While this was all taking place, the actual Slasher was laying low. After lying on the floor next to Elaine Kelly's bed, he wouldn't do anything until January 1959. Though the Ware family of Greenacre were convinced he'd paid a visit to their Juno Parade home, three days before Christmas. It wasn't until Mrs Ware was making the bed at around 8am that she noticed criss-cross cuts in the bedding. Oddly enough, despite there being three people asleep in the room no one woke up or was disturbed by someone slashing the bedsheets they were sleeping underneath.

With the heightened sense of fear causing people to believe the wind rattling their windows was the Slasher trying to make his way inside, it is no surprise that any man seen out and about at night was treated with suspicion. A tennis player walking home from a social game was quizzed by police after someone reported him for wearing sandshoes – the Slasher's choice of footwear – after dark. A garbage worker would face a similar barrage of questions for wearing sandshoes after someone saw a man running from a house with "something on his shoulder".

A young man, who jumped a fence on the way to a tryst with his girlfriend, was spotted by a neighbour who called police. A youth in shorts drew attention for running through the streets of Turrella – his car had run out of petrol and he was rushing to the petrol station before it closed.

A taxi driver noticed the slow pace of a car driving through the streets and grew suspicious it was the Slasher casing the neighbourhood. The police were called and discovered a learner-driver out for practice. Another taxi driver dobbed in a deaf mute man he had taken to a home in the St George area, all because of reports days earlier that a man disturbed in a home seemed to be a deaf.

A girl turned the tables on the taxis, calling the police after a taxi driver she hired began talking about the Slasher in detail. "He seemed to know so much about how the Slasher operated that I got scared," she said. He would be questioned and fingerprinted but they were not a match for the Slasher's.

Canadian Walter Brietze found himself mistaken for the Slasher after catching the wrong train and ending up wandering the empty streets of Birrong about 2am. Despite the suburb being a 15-kilometre drive away from Kingsgrove, his stumbling around looking for a cab drew the attention of the locals.

He wasn't able to find a taxi rank on his own and so started looking for a home where the lights were on, so he could knock and ask for help. By that time the police had already been called, and they soon swarmed around him. "Never before have I been so lonely one minute and so popular the next," he joked to *The Sun*.

"By the time everyone pulled up there must have been about 15 policemen all firing question at me.

After a time they were satisfied he wasn't the Slasher and one of the detectives drove him to a taxi.

23

"Police yesterday appealed to St George district residents to leave the Kingsgrove Slasher to them."
Sun-Herald, December 14, 1958

The press weren't above having a bet each way. After freaking people out with ceaseless Slasher coverage through the last month of 1958 even though his only crime was on December 3, they then admonished people for freaking out. In a story headlined "Slasher hunt hampered by hysteria", *The Telegraph* bemoaned how the public fears were "frustrating" police efforts to catch the Kingsgrove Slasher.

"Trigger-happy mobs armed with anything from double-barrel shotguns to billiard cues, race to every alarm," the story read. "Car radios, tuned to the police wave-length, keep self-styled vigilantes informed of every development in the hunt."

On the same day *The Sun Herald* ran a call from CIB deputy J Parmenter to not engage in vigilante behaviour. "We don't want residents to hinder police in their inquiries," he said. "Someone could be killed or seriously injured if arms are used indiscriminately."

The residents, however, weren't listening. The hysteria being actively stoked by the press saw worried citizens begin to look for ways to protect themselves. Self-defence classes did a roaring trade, as did hardware stores as women bought hammers, axes and lengths of timber to place by the bedside as they slept. While no one had managed to lay a hand on the Slasher in anger, they all swore they'd take a swing at him should he venture into their bedroom.

Others went to more extreme or odd measures in the pursuit of self-preservation. Marguerite Austin, who had suffered the deep cut in her abdomen, had taken to sleeping with a container of pepper on her bedside table – "I'd let him have it right in the face". Another woman, who had four children, was sleeping with a fire extinguisher full of "foam acid" within reach. "I will blind him if he disturbs my household," she said. "I would not have pity if he were blinded. Young children must be protected."

Women would be better off sleeping with open tins of paint next to them, according to Manly doctor Herbert PT Hyde. "Should the occasion arise they could slosh the paint over the intruder." he said. "The paint-soaked clothing might disclose his identity." Mr de Courcy-Gribble came up with a "fluid gun" that would blind the Slasher. The gun included a plastic container that emitted an unstated fluid which would both blind the attacker (though not permanently) and stain his face. He came up with the idea following a series of taxi driver bashings in 1956. "The Slasher and other attackers of women and taxi drivers would have been caught long ago had their victims been equipped with these little weapons," he insisted.

Other more foolish advice offered to police included dialing all but the last digit of the police phone number (on the old rotary dial phones of the 1950s) before going to bed. The person could then tie a thread to hold the rotary dial in place until an intruder entered and tripped on the thread, which would automatically dial the last number and alert the police. No mention was made of what the other end of the thread should be attached to, nor how police were meant to respond when there would be no one at the other end when they picked up the phone. Dye-filled water pistols was another option, as was the sprinkling of dye powder on window sills. Someone also rang the cops to advise that people could also scatter thumb tacks on their lawn "for waiting police to pounce when the Slasher finds one".

While the actual Slasher mightn't have been out and about since December 3, incredibly, other prowlers were. Despite a special taskforce being set up and on patrol each night rushing to each and every prowler call, and despite the residents in the area jumping at shadows every night, some still chanced their arm and went out.

One of those was a crim known as the green car man. In early December there were reports of a male intruder being spotted in houses and making his getaway in a green Holden. The first was on December 4, just a day after the Slasher visited Elaine Kelly. At 12.15am the man was first spotted in a house in Henry Street, Carlton, a suburb to the south of the Slasher zone. A Mr Duncombe said his 18-year-old daughter Carol saw the man staring through her bedroom window as she was undressing. "I turned around and was horrified to see a big, thickly built man standing at the open window and looking straight at me," she said. She slammed the window in his face.

Ten minutes later he was 800 metres away, standing on a flowerpot outside 17-year-old Rhona Dickinson's Shirley Street bedroom, where she was undressing after being on a date with her boyfriend. What she noticed was his hand waving at her through the open window. "I was struck dumb at first," she said. "But I screamed as loud as I could when I saw his head rising over the window sill."

A short while later, he was spotted a kilometre west in Waratah Street, Bexley. In each instance he was seen driving off in a green Holden. Rhona told police she remembered the car driving past several times as her boyfriend was walking her home.

The timing of the incidents led the papers and, for a short while, the police to believe this was their man. If the Slasher had been using a car it would explain how he managed to strike at places as far away as the North Shore (at this stage police weren't aware he had been living over the bridge at the time).

He was back on the road on December 12. About 10pm Kevin Brennan, 18, had just returned to the family home in Hastings Road, Ramsgate – almost eight kilometres southeast of Kingsgrove. Hearing his 19-year-old sister Annette screaming that there was a man in the backyard, he grabbed a knife and raced out to confront him. "I heard a noise in the yard but couldn't see anyone," he said. Meanwhile another sister, Margaret, was at the front door and saw the man drive off at high speed in a green sedan.

Ten days later, buried in another story, *The Mirror* reported that "the man in the green Holden" had been arrested by police. But there appears to be no further reports on who he was or what happened to him.

24

"Six police cars early today went to Hurstville after a man had been disturbed on the verandah of a house in Hurstville Road."
The Telegraph, December 26, 1958

Politicians in the modern era know the importance of being "tough on crime". The voters don't want to see their elected representatives fiddling while Rome starts to burn. So we get increased jail terms for various offences, police ministers putting pressure on the cops to catch crims and the justice minister pushing the legal fraternity to make sure those crims get locked up.

It must have been a different political landscape in the 1950s because Georges River MP Douglas Cross, whose electorate took in the Slasher's territory, seemed in no great hurry to bring up the subject. The Liberal MP won the seat on March 3, 1956, just five days before the Slasher stumbled across Margaret Campbell and her beau parked in the Beverly Hills scrub, and would be the region's MP for the Slasher's entire reign (and beyond, holding it until his death in 1970).

Yet he would wait until after the Slasher had attacked 14 women and children before deciding to mention it in parliament.

"Thousands of people are becoming alarmed indeed," he thundered on December 9, "and many are in a state of nervous tension. This person might be deranged. Some people are of [the] opinion that he has escaped from a mental institution or, having been an inmate, he was released on parole some time ago and did not return."

Conveniently overlooking his own inaction on the issue to date he said the government wasn't doing enough and called on Premier Joseph Cahill to take action. "The occupiers of hundreds of homes in my area are closing their windows and doors at night, though at this time of the year they should have them wide open," he said.

Cahill recognised Cross was just engaging in some political pointscoring, but he would return the following day with a statement from the police commissioner outlining the actions taken by investigating officers.

"A thorough search and examination has been made of each of the premises entered for some evidence which would assist in identification," Cahill told parliament, reading from the statement. "In some cases portions of fingerprints have been found, but in no case has there been found complete fingerprints from which identification could be made. From the fingerprints found, the fingerprint experts have prepared a composite set of fingerprints."

Detectives had also been in touch with police in every state, as well as New Zealand, asking if they were aware of any criminal who may be responsible for these crimes. Offenders on parole from jail or psychiatric hospitals had been investigated to see if any were prone to slashing women in their beds.

Cahill also informed the parliament that any reports of a prowler in the St George area were immediately given top priority. "Special provision has been made at the Police Wireless Section for reports received of persons acting in suspicious circumstances which might indicate that the Slasher is again operating to receive special attention," he said.

"Additional detectives and uniformed police have been performing duty in the area where the attacks have occurred, and four wireless-equipped police vehicles operate in the same area throughout the whole of the night."

Still some residents decided to try and catch the Slasher themselves. One of them was a former British paratrooper Roy Muller, who was living in Kogarah. The man had noticed footprints in his backyard and so set up a stakeout. For four straight nights he pulled on a black tracksuit and hid for hours in bushes in the yard, waiting to pounce.

The prowler did come into the yard on the first few nights of Muller's stakeout but was too far away for the home owner to make a move. On the fourth night – January 12 – it was just a few minutes before midnight and Muller was about to give up and go to bed when he spotted the prowler peeping into a bedroom window.

"I was ready to whack him with a big torch I had ready," an excited Muller told *The Sun*, "but he was just out of reach."

Instead, Muller leapt out from behind the bushes and ran at the figure. "He was off like a shot and although I kept about five feet behind, I couldn't quite close the gap. Just before I lost him he leapt over a six-foot paling fence but he lost his left shoe."

Police ruled out Muller's prowler as being the Slasher. But that man would be out just a week later, on the morning of January 21. The Slasher's 15th attack would be on an 11-year-old girl asleep in bed next to her nine-year-old sister. It would also be the only Slasher crime where someone fought back. Just before dawn on a Wednesday, the Slasher climbed the steep hill of Duff Street,

Arncliffe, just a 350-metre walk from his Park Street home. The Eardley home was at the top of the hill, the last house at the end of the street.

He noticed the streetlight outside the house and made sure to stay clear of it, even though it was 4.30am and dawn was slowly lighting up the sky. The Slasher climbed onto the front verandah, where a window was open slightly. He pushed it open further, but his view of the room inside was blocked by a set of venetian blinds and a blanket hung to block the glare from the streetlight directly outside the house.

Asleep in the room was 11-year-old Helen Downs and her sister Sharon, 9, who were living with their grandparents. The sisters were sharing the room with their aunt, 18-year-old Elaine Eardley, who was about to do what no-one else had managed – land a blow on the Slasher.

The man pushed the blinds and blanket forward, spying the sleeping forms of Helen and her sister just below the window. Despite it being obvious she was just a child, wearing shortie-style summer pajamas, the Slasher still reached in and ran his hand along her body. Putting his hand underneath her pajama top, he groped her chest, squeezing hard.

Sensing something was wrong in the room Elaine woke up. She looked to the front window; at first she noticed they were pushed forward slightly. What she saw next shocked her; a man's arm underneath the blinds, pulling away from Helen's body – Elaine never actually saw him grope the girl.

Some had lay petrified when they saw the Slasher in their bedroom, others screamed for help from their beds. But Elaine was made of sterner stuff. Seeing the arm reaching into her room, she crept out of her bed and picked up one of her high-heeled shoes from the floor. Leaping onto the girls' bed, Elaine yanked away the venetians and came face-to-face with the Slasher.

"Go on, get out!" she yelled, smacking him in the face with her heeled shoe. The man staggered back in shock that someone had fought back and then fled lest the 18-year-old continue to retaliate. Downs herself apparently slept through all this, only waking up when Elaine accidentally stepped on her leg while getting off the bed.

Downs escaped with only two small scratches on her chest and one on her shoulder. Her aunt's intervention likely saved her from falling victim to the Slasher's razor. Though when later asked by police if he would have cut her had he not been disturbed he claimed he couldn't remember whether or not he'd brought a blade with him. Which seems hard to believe given he was called the Slasher.

Perhaps because he was interrupted before he could give full vent to his urges, the Slasher was back out on the streets just a week later. Again he would stay within his own suburb of Arncliffe but his hunting ground on the morning of Wednesday, January 28, wouldn't be just around the corner from his own home.

It would be about two kilometres away, in a small red-brick house located a few doors from the end of Valda Avenue, at the eastern edges of the suburb. It was home for 16-year-old Dale Batger and her family. And after the Slasher arrived in her room at 1.45am it would never quite feel like home again.

Dale was asleep in the room she shared with her 10-year-old sister at the rear of the house. They each slept in a single bed and a third bed lay empty between them. As was the case with a number of the Slasher's victims, Dale's bed was underneath the bedroom window.

The Slasher must have been desperate to get inside for he put in some effort. The bedroom window that overlooked a very slim driveway was too high up the wall for him to climb straight in, so he prowled around looking for something that would help. He found a solution in the yard of the Oldhams next door. He carried eight house bricks from the backyard of their home to the Batgers, which would have taken two, maybe three trips. He stacked them in a small pile and then went back to the neighbour's yard a fourth time to grab a stool he'd seen there.

Placing the stool so the legs sat on the bricks, the Slasher carefully stood on it. He tore out the flyscreen, bending back the nails that held the frame in place. That was dropped on the concrete driveway before he pushed the already-open window all the way up. Dale was sleeping on her side with her back to the window.

Along the window ledge was a money box, some small statues of rabbits and several ornaments Dale had placed there. The Slasher picked them up and placed them in the garden at the side of the house so he wouldn't knock them over as he reached into the window.

He took a razor and made several half-hearted cuts in Dale's pillow, leaving what he'd come to think of as his signature. Putting the razor away, he reached in with both hands, sliding one under her body, so he could grasp her breasts with both hands. He squeezed them so hard Dale woke screaming and slid out of bed in an attempt to get away. But the Slasher hung on, allowing himself to be pulled into the bedroom.

"Mummy!" Dale screamed hysterically. Her mother Joan woke and quickly raced to her daughter's room just in time to see the Slasher, wearing a red pullover, darting out of the bedroom window. Dale lay on the floor, screaming with her face in her hands. Her daughter's summer pajama top was pulled up around her neck and her mother could already make out deep red marks around her breasts from the Slasher's fingers.

Both breasts would later go very dark with bruising and Dale would later tell a courtroom, the skin would start to peel off at the site of the finger marks. She didn't go back to sleep that night, staying awake in the lounge room next to her mother. After the attack she would also find scratches on her face and wrist, and her mouth would be sore, yet she would have no explanation for those injuries. Given the Slasher's previous attacks and his claim to police that "I only wanted to wake her up", it's possible the Slasher punched her in the mouth at some stage. The Slasher would, however, never admit to anything more than the violent groping.

The assault would leave Dale Batger with some serious psychological scars. She would not go out at night without someone accompanying her from door to door, even to the outdoor toilet in broad daylight. In the middle of the day her parents would find her hiding behind the lounge, weeping and shaking, hiding her face in her hands. Several times over the coming months, Joan Batger would call Detective Brian Doyle over to see if he could, in his words, "straighten her out a bit".

Dale was far from alone. A number of the Slasher's victims carried their own scars, physical and psychological. Rosalie Meyer would get crying attacks when she read about the other Slasher victims in the papers and insisted her parents install slasher bars on the windows.

Anne Willis, who was just seven at the time of the Slasher's 1956 assault would wake screaming over the next two years, and come to sleep in a stretcher bed set up in her parents' room. She would be terrified of using the bathroom, fearful of someone climbing down from the manhole in the roof or hiding in the shower recess. A doctor would eventually have to prescribe her sedatives.

Fifteen-year-old Gloria Geyson would still occasionally sleep in her parents' room for several years after her July 1956 attack. Even things like seeing a man in a laneway while walking home would scare her.

Lesley Coleman, who had been punched so hard in the mouth her teeth were broken, refused to be on her own either inside or outside. As well as the scar across her abdomen Marguerite Austin would lose a lot of weight due to the after-effects of the attack and need regular doctor visits. For years after the Slasher's visit Georgina Palmer of McMahons Point refused to sleep in that bedroom. Elaine Eardley would need tablets to get to sleep at night.

While none of them could know it in January 1959, the Slasher's reign of terror was coming to an end. The police would capture him in just three months' time. But that would still be too late to save a 72-year-old woman and a 14-year-old girl.

25

"The Slasher appears to have knowledge of every piece of bushland, every stormwater canal and drain and areas where escape is easy."
Daily Mirror, February 11, 1959

For that relief to come, the police had to catch the Slasher, which they had realised was a difficult thing to do. He was a cleanskin with no fingerprints on file so the composite Slasher prints they had wouldn't help focus the investigation on a single suspect. There were even media reports that the police had gone on a door-to-door canvass of Slasher territory, asking to take the fingerprints of every male between the ages of 15 and 45. A canvass which did not bear fruit because it apparently stopped just two streets short of the Slasher's front door.

He had no criminal record and connections to the underworld, so the well-worn method of getting one crim to dob in another would not help the police find their man.

All the investigating that could be done, had been done. Police had already questioned hundreds of people, which included any male out after the sun went down.

In a report to his superiors, Detective Doyle added a list of the vast range of people investigated by the team:

"PMG linesmen, water board workers, electricity linesmen ... milkmen, grocers delivering, bakers, butchers delivering, time payment collectors, dry cleaners, electrical repairers, painters, plaster repairers, plumbers, house repairers, television demonstrators ... telephone mechanics, lino and carpet layers, doctors calling, electricity meter readers, furniture delivery men, insurance collectors, rent collectors, fumigators, gas appliance men, ambulance collectors, laundry collectors, lawn cutters, radio repairers, upholsterers, vacuum cleaner repairers, visitors from church bodies and clergy."

So Doyle figured the only way to stop the Slasher would be to catch him in the act. With the help of Jeffrey Eardley, the father of Elaine, Doyle devised a plan that would eventually crack the case at the end of April. Shrouded by bushland the Wolli Creek runs through the centre of the Slasher zone. Doyle had come to believe the Slasher was using the bush to cross from the southern suburbs to those in the north, as well as to escape unseen. Eardley, a keen bushwalker and birdwatcher, knew the bush tracks and drew a map for Doyle, showing the tracks and trails a man could use to cut through the bush.

"As it transpired," Doyle would write to his superiors, "it proved to be a plan of the entire action of the night of the arrest ... it was just as if the plan had been prepared months in advance of what was to happen."

Using the map, Doyle came up with an unusual plan for his Slasher Patrol. Doyle had grabbed fit young officers from 21 Division, Vice Squad and elsewhere to join his team. After a few weeks of patrolling the streets, Doyle decided they would have to head bush, and the Eardley map was part of that plan.

"Men were specially trained for this job," Doyle would explain at the Slasher's trial, "and placed in positions for many months in various parts of the scrub and swampland in the vicinity of Turrella, Bardwell Park and Undercliffe."

"Whole areas were planned and mapped out and use was made of special aerial maps of the suburbs."

The Slasher Patrol would be split into groups and given names. The Lovers – with one male officer in drag – would sit together in cars or linger in quiet laneways that the Slasher might use. The Racers were behind the wheel of fast cars ready to move when the alarm of another strike was sounded. And then there was the dreaded Commandos. Dreaded by the officers themselves, that is. Referred to as "Siberia" the commandos had to spend the night in the bush and swampland, a particularly unpleasant job when the weather would turn cold and wet.

Part of Doyle's strategy was to create different plans for each suburb the Slasher may visit. So there was the Turrella Plan, the Arncliffe Plan, the Earlwood Plan, the Banksia Plan among others. When the alarm sounded, the men of Slasher Patrol would know what to do.

And while Doyle's plans would put pressure on the Slasher, the razor man wasn't quite done yet. At just seven years old, Anne Willis was the Slasher's youngest victim. In the early hours of February 11, 1959, he would find his oldest – 72-year-old Mona Sumner.

She lived in Slade Road, Bardwell Park, with her son and his family, on a corner with a laneway that ran north to the rail line just behind her house. Today shops occupy the laneway opposite the house, but in 1959 it was all bushland. Unlike today, there was no high wall blocking access to the rail line and – unfortunately for Sumner – the Wolli Creek bush immediately across the tracks.

At 2.30am on that Wednesday, Sumner was asleep in one of the side rooms that overlook the laneway. The low wooden fence that ran down the lane and close to the house made it easy for anyone walking down the lane to look right into the windows. Sumner had been diagnosed with thrombosis just a few days earlier and was largely confined to her bed.

A *Mirror* photographer managed to convince Sumner to pose for a photo in that bed after the attack. The photo, which would appear on the front page of that afternoon's edition shows Sumner lying down and pretending to sleep, her glasses still on her face. Behind her in the photo are the curtains covering the window the Slasher had used. The window is so close to the bed that he again could have attacked his victim without having to enter the room.

Which is exactly what the Slasher did. Wielding a dull penknife he'd sharpened that day rather than his usual razor, the Slasher tore out the flyscreen and removed a few items – a jar of ointment, a glass tumbler – that had been left on the window sill. He stretched his right arm across Sumner's sleeping body.

He slashed her blankets and nightdress, leaving her with a six-centimetre cut over her breasts. Sumner would wake while the attack was happening, disturbed by the tearing noise of the dull penknife cutting through her sheets.

"An arm stretched against my body and all I could see was the shape of a man," she told *The Mirror*. "His arm moved and something began slashing my clothing, something very sharp. I felt a stinging on my body."

She screamed out for help, which stopped the Slasher in his tracks. "The scream might have saved me from being cut again," she suggested. Just two days later, her son would install slasher bars over her bedroom window.

Doyle and his Slasher Patrol rushed to the scene on Wednesday morning, ordering in police dogs to see if they could pick up the Slasher's scent. Doyle ended up appearing in a photo for *The Mirror*'s front page story (headlined "Slasher's 17th victim", in five-centimetre-high capitals), his hand inside the glass tumbler as he inspected it for a possible print. Later that day Doyle would explain to *The Sun* what he thought was driving the Slasher.

"From intense probing we believe he is an egoist trying to show just what damage he could do if he wanted to. In all the attacks he has never appeared to want badly to wound his victim."

Psychiatrist Dr McGeorge would also return to the media coverage to push his mistaken view of the Slasher's hatred of women. "I believe he is a man who keeps to himself, shuns company and has no women friends," he said of a man who was married and well-liked by others. The good doctor also believed the serial attacker was an "athletic type", a conclusion that could be made by anyone with a brain in their head.

The Slasher's next attack – which would also turn out to be his last – would give Dr McGeorge and those in his field plenty to work with.

26

"His attack proved conclusively that he is a pervert."
Daily Telegraph, February 13, 1959

The night of the Slasher's final attack would be a busy one for the man. By his own later admission to police he was out "for the best part of the night". It was barely 48 hours after his assault on Mona Sumner but he needed to head out again.

So he headed to Highcliff Road in Earlwood. It offered a perfect escape route; even today most of the street only has houses on one side, the other side is taken up by that Wolli Creek bush. Were someone to see him and a quick getaway was needed, he could just dart into undergrowth and disappear along a nearby walking track.

And someone did see him. After spending a few hours getting inside a number of houses in the street, an elderly couple disturbed a man in a red jumper acting suspiciously in a neighbour's driveway. The Slasher bolted for the bush while the pair called police, who could find no sign of the man. That was because, by the time they arrived, he had already made his way east along a track through the bush corridor and was in Banks Road, about 800 metres away.

Once there he picked up where he left off – "having a look around" as he would put it. "I suppose I would have been in nearly every house in Banks Road that night," he later told police. And the only one where someone spotted him was the last – the home of 14-year-old Helen Gaffey. Unlike his other recent attacks, where he was disturbed quite quickly, the Slasher took his time at the Gaffeys' Banks Road home. The Slasher Patrol would have to spend a good deal of time piecing together the sequence of events that led up to him climbing into the room Helen shared with her nine-year-old sister at the rear of the house.

The Slasher would find a small table on the back porch. Lifting it with both hands, he carried down to Helen's window. He then went back to the porch for a wooden fruit box he had seen. Looking for a way to get into the window which had the sill at head height, he placed the box on top of the table. Testing the structure, he found it too shaky for his liking and moved it away.

The yard had an outhouse which included a laundry. The Slasher managed to break in and discovered an eight-rung stepladder that would do the trick. With some paint rags he found on the porch tied at the top to muffle any sound, he placed the ladder against the wall outside Helen's bedroom.

The flyscreen was held in place by a few drawing pins, which were easily removed. That enabled him to reach inside and open the window, shifting a bottle of ink and some ornaments to the far edge of the window sill. And then he climbed in.

Rather than go straight to work, he picked up a dish of flowers and took them out of the room. Creeping through the darkened house, he chocked open the back door and the took the flowers down the rear yard near the back fence.

Returning to Helen's room he scooped up a pile of clothing she'd left in a box – pants, bra, underwear, and slip – and took them into the back yard. There, under the moonlight he violently tore them to pieces with his hands, leaving the shredded clothing on the grass. After that he returned to wake up Helen.

Standing at her bedside, the Slasher reached under Helen's sheets and groped the teen's breasts, squeezing viciously. Still half asleep, Helen grabbed the Slasher's arm as he fought to get free, dragging her out of the bed. He managed to break free just as Helen screamed out "Mummy! Daddy!". He darted out the window before her parents arrived to find Helen sobbing that a man had been in her room.

They took her into their bedroom and called the police. That was when her mother noticed the marks and bruising on her breast, which would darken and peel just as they would with Dale Batger. Aside from that injury, Helen would have just a few scratches from the Slasher's fingernails. Even mentally she seemed to avoid any scars, Doyle describing her at the trial as "a very sensible little girl who recovered quickly and suffered no great after-effects of shock at all."

The Mirror went into full outrage mode on the front page for Friday, February 13. The massive headline read "18! Yes, the Slasher struck again last night. An appalling record by the police". The story criticised the police for being unable to capture this "obviously mentally deranged and dangerous" criminal.

"During this whole period of terror there is no record of a single policeman having got out of a car and chased a suspect," *The Mirror* inaccurately ranted.

"Why are there no police on the beat? Can it be true that after two and a half years the police still have no clue?"

The "latest outrage" scored a further two pages inside, which included photos of the ladder propped under the bedroom window, police quizzing neighbours and footprints left on a concrete path which the paper was certain were left by the Slasher.

The coverage inside laid the boot into the police even further, claiming Doyle's approach was all wrong. Forget an elite squad, all that was needed to catch the Slasher was police walking a beat. Everywhere. At the same time.

"A systematic patrol of the entire area of attack by foot police is the only solution," Earlwood P&C president Mr Swindale said.

Canterbury Mayor Alderman S Squires felt there was nothing a cop walking the streets couldn't solve.

"What we want is the man on the beat and not the flying squad," he said. "The old foot-slogger is a far greater deterrent to the potential criminal than a fleet of police cars."

Walter Lawrence, MP for the seat of Drummoyne (which, oddly, doesn't seem be to the location any of the 18 Slasher attacks) also swore by the copper wearing out his shoe leather.

"What we need is more police on the beat, getting around gathering local information," he said. "The old-time man on the beat knew and talked to everyone in his district and collected apparently inconsequential information which later turned out to be vital leads."

Doyle's boss CIB head Calman, launched an appeal for information from the public on the very same day as the 18th attack. This was despite the police already being deluged by information from the public.

In what seems like a slight at the work of his own officers, Calman said "An extraordinary number of detectives have been working night and day in the Slasher districts but, so far, they have been unable to find any clue to his identity.

"From dusk last night, one of the largest special patrols ever to be instituted in Sydney started. It will be maintained until the Slasher is run to earth."

It wouldn't – an apparent lack of immediate results would see the numbers on the Slasher case wound down rather than increased. Doyle was getting hit from all sides; he was being criticised in the press, his bosses were questioning his approach and local worthies who had high opinions of themselves rang him to offer their less-than-helpful tips on how to catch the Slasher. In February 1959 Doyle moved himself to permanent night shift until the Slasher was caught. But during the day when he was trying to sleep, the calls kept coming. So he disconnected the phone, hired a housekeeper to help his wife look after their five children and slept next door. The stress and overwork saw him lose 10 kilograms. But he was on the right track. Three years of information from the public had led nowhere. A cop walking a beat wasn't going to scare away the Slasher. The criminal wasn't going to be identified until he was caught.

Though Doyle didn't know it, his work had already stopped the Slasher. The attack on Gaffey would be the Slasher's last and his new plan to have his men lurk in the Wolli Creek bush would put the pressure on the Slasher, leading to two police pursuits before his capture just over two months after he leapt from Helen Gaffey's bedroom.

27

"We are dealing with an opponent who has repeatedly proved his elusiveness."
CIB Supt MF Calman, *Telegraph*, February 13, 1959

The Slasher's reign may have finished with the attack on Helen Gaffey, but other women would come forward with dubious claims to be victims as well. In February a 17-year-old cub mistress by the name of Elva Seller would be, in the words of *The Mirror*, "slashed about the face and neck".

That was overstating things a bit; she wasn't slashed at all but attacked with a wire brush. Apparently her assailant ran the wire brush across her face. But a look at the photo taken the day of the incident is very dubious; all the marks appear quite superficial, as though whoever did it was hoping to avoid inflicting any pain. Most of the marks are also quite short in length, and straight, suggesting the person's face was still when they were made. It's hard to accept that there was *any* attacker, rather that the cub mistress lightly scratched her own face with the wire brush. Why she would choose to do that is anyone's guess, but Detective Doyle would state in court that police would have to respond to a number of bogus calls.

Glen Humphries

The case of Penshurst teen Diana Worsley likely fits into this category as well. In late February she would claim to be slashed at home twice in the space of eight days, which newspapers hungry for anything that sounded like the Slasher lapped up.

The first incident involving the 15-year-old Worsley occurred in the backyard of her family's home. Her family was away on holiday but she had returned home on February 15, a Sunday night, to go to school the next morning. The only other person at home that Sunday night was her grandmother.

Diana told police she was outside hanging her school blouse on the clothesline when the man struck, cutting her lightly on the face three times (cuts which are all but impossible to see in any photos of her published by the newspaper). He had been hiding in some bushes before attacking her, and then leapt over the back fence. In what sounds like an act of staging, there was also an upturned bin outside Diana's bedroom. So just where was the attacker? Was he standing on the bin at the window, or was he hiding in the bushes in the backyard?

The second incident took place in Diana's bedroom just over a week later on Monday, February 23. Diana shared a double bed with her nine-year-old sister Jean. That night Jean didn't hear or feel a thing, until 11.30pm.

"I wakened with a start when I heard Diana scream," Jean told the *Telegraph* reporter. "I started to scream and my stepfather ran into our room.

"When he put on the light I saw Diana lying trembling alongside me. I saw blood on her face and chest and thought she was dead."

Diana had what police reported as "scratches" on her face and chest, while Jean – sleeping right next to her – suffered nothing more than a small cut to her pajamas. There was also a trail of torn clothing from the girls' bedroom to the bathroom. Oddly, Diana's dog did not bark at any intruder in the yard that night, and police could not find any sign of how someone might have entered the house. Which means it was likely an "inside job", and that both of the claimed attacks were actually staged.

In between those two questionable "attacks" on Diana Worsley, the Slasher Patrol almost got their man. Just five nights after he took his time at the Gaffey house, the Slasher was out again, 200 metres away from Tabrett Street, the focal point for Slasher hysteria just three months earlier. Blanche Wigmore spotted his arm reaching through the bedroom window of her Highclere Avenue home in Rockdale. She screamed to her husband, who rushed into the room and looked out the window to see the Slasher racing down their driveway.

The Wigmores called police but, as they headed to the couple's house, another call over the radio diverted them. Ralph Lovett was sitting in his truck, parked a block away in Eve Street, when he turned on his headlights and caught a man running towards an unmade road that cut through Barton Park. Still to this day, the park has a large strip of bushland running north-south for more than half a kilometre, much of which brushes up against suburban streets in Banksia and Arncliffe.

Between 14 and 20 police cars – depending on which newspaper you believe – surrounded the park and officers began to search the bush and a stormwater canal that cut the park in two, running east-west from Banksia to empty into Muddy Creek at Kyeemagh.

Unbeknownst to police at the time, they had the Slasher trapped for a while. Doyle's plan to attack the bush was paying off; the Slasher began to feel trapped within the park. The high police turnout had him panicking because he could not see a way out. He had to take cover in the scrub, hiding from pursuing police in the hope an avenue of escape would present itself. In the end, after several hours of evading capture, he found a stormwater channel and followed it east to Kyeemagh. It was the opposite direction from his Arncliffe home but it got him out of the enclosing police net.

The near capture would frighten the Slasher so much that he vowed to slow things down, "only doing one now and then to keep the hunt up", as he would later tell police during almost 24 hours of questioning.

Meanwhile, in another sign that the politicians weren't quick to respond to the Slasher, on February 25 Premier JJ Cahill officially signed off on a £1000 reward. That decision came several weeks after the Slasher committed his last attack and a whopping three years since he began with Margaret Campbell in March 1956.

The reward notice, which went up in more than 500 police stations in NSW and others in Brisbane and Melbourne, cut short the Slasher's period of activity to July-December 1956 and November 1958 to February 1959. That suggested that, even at this stage, police had not connected the Slasher's assault on Campbell as she sat in a car in the Beverly Hills scrub with a boyfriend or the March 1958 attack on Robin Williams, where he seemed to want to choke the girl, to their investigation.

"On some occasions the intruder had entered the bedrooms of female occupants in the dwelling houses," the notice read, "and with a sharp instrument cut the bed clothing on the bed occupied by the females and the night attire which they were wearing, in some instances inflicting serious injury upon the females.

"Extensive and exhaustive police investigations have failed to establish the identity of the person or persons responsible for these attacks."

Night Terrors

The reward would be useless in catching the Slasher. Instead, it would be the oft-maligned police who would bring him down. Though one resident would make a play for that £1000 reward.

28

"He's done a terrific lot of mental harm in this district – that's the most shocking part of the whole thing."
Rockdale Council Alderman RK Hislop, *Sun Herald*, March 19, 1959

Not every prowler and peeping Tom looking to take to the streets under cover of darkness was interested in women. At least one – a "swarthy-looking man" – chose to leer at men getting undressed. One of those men was 22-year-old William Sharp, who lived in Unwin Street, Bexley – just a few hundred metres south of the Slasher's preferred stomping ground.

Just what happened on the night of March 25 – including whether or not Sharp was wearing pants – varies depending on which paper you read. The more lurid version, which appeared in *The Mirror* and *Telegraph*, had the grocer changing for bed after arriving home from the movies at midnight. He then spied the man looking at him through the bedroom window.

Sharp decided to give chase – perhaps without pants if *The Mirror*'s reporting is to be believed. "Clad only in a singlet Sharp ran from the room, out a back door and into the yard."

However, Sharp told *The Sun* he was in bed when he heard a noise from a window in the kitchen, not the bedroom.

"I got out of bed, went to the window to investigate and got the shock of my life to see a swarthy-looking man staring me straight in the face," he told the reporter.

"I called out to him to stay where he was but he jumped down from a pushbike propped against the wall that he was standing on and raced down the backyard."

This time Sharp was wearing pajamas when he gave chase, leaping fences and running through backyards before the peeping Tom hit scrubland and disappeared.

While he lived in Arncliffe the Slasher had established a routine. At home on the morning of a day he planned to go prowling, he would tell his wife not to expect him home as he would be working late. At the end of the day he would leave work at the usual time, carrying his prowling get-up in his bag. He'd ride the train to Turrella, which was his usual stop.

Instead of walking south towards his Park Street, Arncliffe home, he headed north over the train line to a footbridge at the end of Henderson Street. The footbridge gave him access to his beloved Wolli Creek bushland.

Once he was safely in the bush, away from the streets and houses and the possibility of being spotted, the Slasher would change out of his work clothes and into the pullover, trousers and rubber-soled sandshoes for prowling. His street clothes he would leave in the bush until he had satisfied his urges, then he would return for them. Except for the early hours of March 12 when he had to leave his bag in the bush near Turrella, because he was too busy trying to escape from Doyle's commandos who were chasing him through the bush.

The prowling that night lasted for about eight hours and is an indication of what he did before he slashed all those women. The Slasher didn't wander the dark streets, peering up at the houses he past until he decided to give into an urge and break into one, where there just happened to be a female asleep inside.

No, he would spend the night climbing into people's houses and creeping around, using some mysterious inner clock to decide when the lurking was over and the slashing could begin. He told police that, before he attacked Helen Gaffey in February he'd been in almost every other house in her street, but no one but Helen had woken and spotted him.

This seemed something the residents in the Slasher zone never realised; if he'd attacked a woman in your street, there was a very good chance he'd been in your house earlier that night. He may have stood at the foot of your bed and watched you sleeping. Perhaps he sat in that armchair in the corner of the lounge room, the one that would give him an ideal view of anyone walking down the hall to use the toilet.

He may even have slipped into your children's bedroom to see if there were any young women there who took his fancy. Maybe he bent over and picked up some underwear or other item of clothing from the floor to take with him; the next day people would wake, be unable to find it and scratch their heads as to what happened to it. At the man's trial there was mention of other minor offences like trespass and theft that police chose not to charge him with. The theft may have related to his taking "souvenirs" from various houses.

On March 11, the Slasher got off the train and headed into the bush to get changed. Then he headed back to one of his favourite streets – Highcliff Road in Earlwood. The street ran parallel to Bayview Avenue, where in 1956 he climbed into the bedroom of

Rosalie Meyer and hit her in the face with a lump of wood. It was also the same street where an elderly couple rousted him, forcing the Slasher down to Banks Road and the home of his last victim. And the southern side of the street was bushland, which provided an easy getaway. Just a few steps across the road and he would be gone.

He would later tell police he was very busy on the evening of March 12. "I would have been in dozens and dozens of houses that night," he said, "but I don't think anyone got onto me apart from the girl and her father in Highcliff Road.

He was referring to the North family. After being in dozens of houses in her street, the Slasher was sprung by a 21-year-old cub mistress named Barbara North (*The Mirror*, up to its old tricks, referred to her as "a most attractive girl"). When she'd gone to bed North had closed her bedroom window to a chilly wind blowing. At around 4am, the cool shiver of a breeze in her room woke her. Looking at the window, she could see it was now wide open and the wire screen had been removed. Bravely creeping closer, she got close enough to look out the window – there was a man crouched on the verandah under the sill.

"Help me, dad!" she screamed, as the Slasher jumped the railing along the verandah (in a "Tarzan-like fashion", according to *The Mirror*), through the front gate he had left open and across the road to the bush.

"Instead of running into mud flats and into a creek, as anyone ignorant of the layout of the ground might have done, the Slasher dived down a narrow track which took him to Turrella railway station," said *The Mirror*.

North had seen enough of the Slasher to give the police who came to her home the following description; "solid build, 5ft 10 to 6ft, dressed in fawn trousers and probably wearing rubber-soled shoes". Fleeing the scene, the Slasher headed south through the bush as he had done so many times before, heading towards the footbridge over the swamp at Turrella. Once he made it there, he had a look over his shoulder; perhaps he could still see a few torchlights in the scrub back at Highcliff Road, maybe he could hear the shouts of searchers crashing through the bush. One thing was certain, he figured he'd given police the slip. So he slowed his pace to a walk, confidently strolling through the pre-dawn streets of Turrella – most likely heading to his house just a suburb away.

But things would be different this time. Detective Doyle, together with Jeffrey Eardley, reckoned they'd figured out the Slasher's escape routes – through the bush and out the other side. So, when he'd rushed into the undergrowth at Earlwood, the Slasher Patrol's plan went into action. They expected him to pop up at Turrella – the footbridge was the easiest point to cross over – so at least one car crawled those suburban streets.

And it paid off. Detective Constables Lynch and Gorman were cruising along Turrella Street, when they spied the Slasher ambling along, full of certainty that he was smarter than the police and had gotten away.

When the car was less than 20 metres away, the Slasher noticed them and darted off into bushland again. The two constables called for assistance and dove into the bush themselves. Soon more than a dozen officers arrived to help the search, standing shoulder-to-shoulder as they bashed through the bush while spotlights lit up the area, even though it was dawn. Other detectives headed to a group of huts in the bush known locally as "Happy Valley", where itinerants and homeless people camped. There they rousted the residents to see if anyone answering the Slasher's description was among them.

The Slasher wasn't at Happy Valley and with dawn breaking, and a light rain starting to fall, police called off the search through the bush. But there would be two things that came out the early morning chase. One was the realisation that the Doyle plan could well be the difference. And the second would be that it would cause some concern for the Slasher; a focus on the bushland meant the police had figured out where he would go when a home owner caught him inside their house. And if they knew where he was going to be, it became that much easier for the police to catch him.

29

"Some members of my church have been his victims and there is no doubt that someone will be killed if this continues."
Kingsgrove Church of England Revered Weir, *Daily Mirror*,
March 13, 1959

The night after that close call, the Slasher didn't "work late". He was at home with his wife, reading the evening newspapers which were full of the news of his escape. The Slasher wasn't a subject to be avoided in the man's own house. Just a few weeks earlier they were sitting together at home, when she read out something from a newspaper story about the Slasher.

"What sort of a chap do you think the Slasher is?" she asked, not aware she actually already knew the Slasher.

"Whoever he is, he would be the greatest so and so on earth," he replied. "But don't worry, I'm sure the police will catch him in the end."

Though she continued to worry, so much so that the Slasher had to fit special locks on all the windows and doors in their small Arncliffe flat (there were later media reports that he had to install slasher bars but the man himself makes no mention of that).

That night after his escape, while flicking through the tabloids he came across a story about a plea from the state health minister Bill Sheahan. If the Slasher were to give himself up the minister would work to ensure he got the medical attention he obviously needed.

"The Slasher needs help," Sheahan said. "Now is the time for him to get it, before it's too late."

"I cannot make any promises but I would certainly discuss the matter with Mr Downing [attorney-general Reg Downing] if the Slasher gave himself up and stopped this reign of terror."

It was a fruitless effort; the Slasher had no intention of handing himself into police. He was going to continue his razor work until the law caught up with him, though he didn't think that was ever going to happen.

An unnamed Macquarie Street psychiatrist didn't expect the Slasher to waltz into his local police station either. "I personally feel this man will never give himself up," he told *The Mirror*. "Yesterday's narrow escape will have one of two effects on him. It might frighten him off completely or give him super confidence. Having gotten away in such difficult circumstances he might be more daring than ever."

The Mirror's story about Sheahan's plea also sought the opinion of US evangelist Billy Graham, who happened to be touring Australia at the time. The American promised he would pray for the Slasher.

"If that man would open his heart to God he would be saved," Graham said. "His personal problem would be solved and his terrible urge to mutilate – to sin – would disappear."

But the Slasher didn't have salvation on his mind. He was worried about the bag of work clothes left in the bush when he had to hightail it from police. He didn't want the police stumbling across the clothes, just in case they offered up valuable clues to his identity.

Night Terrors

30

"Property valuations in the area have dropped dramatically, many people have moved from the district and estate agents have reported difficulty in selling houses."
Woman's Day, April 20, 1959

The Slasher wasn't the most popular person in the Kingsgrove area – though one unnamed businessman involved in the chamber of commerce reportedly saw it as great publicity. The way he saw it, now everyone in the state, if not the country, had heard of the suburb thanks to its most infamous resident.

One of the many subsets of Slasher haters were the young men and women in the area. For them, the shadowy figure was a real crimp on their social life. Thanks to the Slasher, parents weren't letting their teenage daughters out at night, much to the dismay of young men like 21-year-old Barry Harris, who lived in Slade Road at Bardwell Park – the same street as victim Mona Sumner.

He preferred to drive around at night rather than walk so as to avoid being stopped by police patrols and being quizzed about where he had been.

"He is a little doleful about the cessation of social life," wrote *Woman's Day* reporter Noel Ottaway.

"You don't see the girls in the quiet streets at night, he says, and at the dances the number of girls had decreased radically and those that go leave early."

Twenty-year-old Robyn Miller – whom Ottaway described as "pretty" – was one of those girls who did still go to dances. Though the likes of Barry had little chance of hooking up as her mother Mary would walk to the train station to meet her and escort her home safely.

The Mirror also focused on a young 20-year-old Slade Road resident by the name of Margot O'Connor – a "slim, brown-eyed girl" – to show the justifiable over-protection parents extended to their daughters. If she was catching the train home after dark her parents would drive to the station, just a seven-minute walk away, to pick her up. Though Margot herself didn't seem too bothered by that.

"I just think it's sensible to take care, and so do my parents," she said. "They don't expect me to come to any harm but they want to be sure."

An unnamed private secretary (her looks are not described by *The Mirror*) was so frightened she never left the house at night without a male escort. Literally – her front yard was heavy with shrubbery and so she dared not walk down the path to the front gate alone. "If social life means staying out after dark and coming home alone, I will just have to go without," she said.

In just a matter of weeks, the fearful secretary and others would be able to leave their homes of an evening because the object of their fears would be behind bars. Though the extended period of quiet since the Slasher's March 12 near-capture wasn't good for the tabloids' circulation figures. And so the absence of the Slasher became the story. Five weeks later – and just 11 days before the serial criminal was captured – *The Mirror* wondered whether he'd done a runner. Despite extended periods between attacks not being unusual for the Slasher *The Mirror* claimed police were investigating the possibility he had left the state or even the country. A third, more logical, option was also floated – that he was lying low until the police pressure eased.

"It could be that he is leading the life he must do outside his slashing complex – that of any normal man who goes to work each day and lives quietly with a wife and family," *The Mirror* reported.

The tabloid was right on the mark – the Slasher was cooling his heels, working a day job and coming home to the wife each night. But on the night of Thursday, April 30, he decided it was time to head out into the night again, just to remind everyone he was still around. He would make it back home that night to see his wife – but he would be wearing handcuffs.

31

"Police early this morning detained a prowler in Finlays Avenue, Earlwood, after a series of dramatic incidents."
Sydney Morning Herald, May 1, 1959

On the morning of May 30, the Slasher sat at the breakfast table across from his wife and told her he'd be working late.

"At least until 11 or even a bit after," he told her. "So don't expect me home until about quarter to midnight."

Saying goodbye, he left their small home in Park Street, Arncliffe, and walked the 800 metres to Turrella Station. Catching a train into town, he likely rode it to Town Hall station, then got off and walked the 350 metres through the CBD to 32 Market Street, then the offices of electrical engineers AW Kemp and Co.

The Slasher had worked for the firm since he left school in the mid-1940s. His job didn't entail electrical work, but rather warehousing and storage duties. Other businesses would store their goods in the warehouse, including a medical supply company and he had once taken it upon himself to steal a few scalpels so he could try them out for himself.

Night Terrors

At around 5.30pm he clocked off for the day, having never planned to work late – at least not in the warehouse. It was a pleasant day for the end of autumn; the afternoon temperatures sitting at a comfortable 22 degrees and no sign of rain in the skies. On the way back to Town Hall station, he stopped in at a Chinese restaurant for dinner (in a sign of the casual racism of the era he would tell police "I went to the chows and had a feed"). Once he'd eaten his fill, the Slasher climbed onto a train and rode it for five stops, disembarking at Turrella station.

The train station on the East Hills line was at the epicentre of his latest crime spree. Leaving out the Elaine Kelly attack, if you were to mark the locations of all his attacks since Marguerite Austin in November and then join them together in an oval, you'd find the train station sat pretty much in the centre.

Incidentally, Rosalie Meyer's house in Undercliffe is the only other victim who lived within that oval; the Slasher was living on the North Shore at the time in November 1956 when he climbed in her window and bashed her with a lump of wood. This suggests he may have used the train station back then to access his hunting ground.

By the time he arrived at Turrella on April 30, it was 7.40pm – the sun had fallen more than two hours ago and darkness had set in. He didn't head south towards his home but north across the railway bridge and into Henderson Street. At the end of the street was a small white wooden footbridge that led into the Wolli Creek bushland he had come to know like the back of his hand.

Once secreted in the bush, he pulled a change of clothes from the bag he had been carrying – trousers, a red pullover and rubber-soled shoes. He headed through the bush to Earlwood, and started prowling. He held off trying to enter any houses because it was not even 9pm; far too early. People would still be awake and, after all these years, he still didn't want to risk capture. But at 10.30pm, he felt the time was right. He was creeping around Finlays Avenue, one of the Earlwood streets that rubs right up against the bush. Freda Grafton was in her bedroom and noticed a man's hand reaching in through the window. She screamed, and her husband dialed the police number – B030 – that every resident no doubt now knew by heart.

Police rushed to the scene and began interviewing Mrs Grafton. Before they could really get into it, there was another call on the radio. Someone had spotted a man lurking in his neighbour's passageway, near a window. The home was in Arncliffe Street, which ran parallel to the street the police were standing in.

Two calls almost on top of each other and just a block apart, it had to be the Slasher. Police rushed round to the new address, but the Slasher could feel the heat and slunk back into the bush. He eventually jumped onto a sewer pipe that poked out of the south side of the bush at Bardwell Park.

Crossing the train lines, he figured the safe bet was to make his way home while the police were occupied on the other side of the bush. So he ran up May Street and planned to make his way through the Bardwell Park streets to his own house. But something happened that forced him to change his plans, something that would end up pushing him into the arms of the Slasher Patrol waiting in the bush.

At the end of the street, he saw a group of men and women standing about. Figuring he would raise suspicion if he ran past them, the Slasher turned around and backtracked along the rail line and over the sewer pipe. He ended up on the northern side of the Wolli Creek gully, but still in bushland rather than back on the suburban streets of Earlwood.

Picking up his bag with his work clothes that he'd hidden just a few hours ago, he made his way along a bush track that curved around Nanny Goat Hill. A large, steep sandstone outcrop that abuts the southern edge of Finlays Avenue, eight years later it would become an environmental hotspot when the government wanted to level it for runway fill at Sydney airport. Earlwood residents objected and, as part of their protest they climbed the steep slopes – the women wearing heels, pearls and carrying handbags – to the top. And they ended up winning, the local council choosing not to allow the blasting that would have leveled the hill.

Back on the last night of April 1959, the Slasher Patrol's Detective Constable Dallas Monley was perched on the hill ready to put one of the plans into action. At about 11.30pm Const Monley spotted the crouched figure of a man darting through the bush in the direction of the footbridge at Turrella.

The constable picked up the walkie-talkie he'd been given (they were a new-fangled gadget at the time) and radioed an urgent message to other members of the patrol. Monley and his partner, Detective Constable Harmer then gave chase through the bush.

At the southern end, two other Slasher Patrol detectives – Gaffney and Sadlier – put their part of the plan into play. They crossed the footbridge, looking to hem the Slasher in. The running man was by now close to the footbridge himself. Seeing the two detectives racing over the bridge and heading towards him, the Slasher veered to the right, hoping against hope to make his way through the swamp without being captured.

Once he was on firm ground on the other side, he was sure his speed – honed from years of athletic meetings – would allow him to escape. But the two detectives were having none of that. Gaffney and Sadlier, along with the rest of the Slasher Patrol, had spent endless nights in and around this stretch of suburban bushland, getting soaked by the rain, being bitten by the mosquitos. Now, with the man who was the reason they'd suffered through that just metres away, there was no way he was escaping.

So the two detectives launched themselves into the muddy swamp under the footbridge. Battling water up to their thighs, they finally laid hands on the man who had evaded the grasp of police for just over three years.

On went the cuffs, moments before Detective Sergeant Doyle arrived. He looked at his wet detectives and then at the man in handcuffs between them. He took in this innocuous figure in a red jumper, looking nothing like the heinous monster many had expected. Were it not for a nose that seemed slightly off-centre and ears that stuck out just a little bit too much, his looks were those of a B-grade movie actor. He certainly didn't look like a man who got his thrills from climbing into women's bedrooms armed with a razor.

"I am Detective Sergeant Doyle," he said to the prisoner. "What is your name?"

The man answered a question with a question – "Are you the officer in charge?"

"Yes."

"I am your man. I am the Kingsgrove Slasher."

It was over.

32

"SLASHER CAUGHT SAY POLICE"
Daily Mirror's front page headline, May 1, 1959

D oyle wanted to make sure what the prisoner said was true. So he called over Senior Constable Gorman of the CIB's fingerprint section. Since the start of the Slasher Patrol, Doyle travelled with a man who knew the criminal's prints. Gorman looked at the man's fingers by torchlight and confirmed to Doyle what the man said was true. They had the Slasher. And they quickly discovered his identity – he was David Joseph Scanlon.

The news quickly went out over the police radio. "This is the message you've all been waiting to hear. The Kingsgrove Slasher has been caught." The police headed to Kogarah station, where Scanlon would be questioned by police through to dinner time the following evening – around 16 hours. There was one pause around 2pm to take him to the courthouse next-door to appear before a magistrate. There was also an earlier pause, around two hours after his capture.

Scanlon's wife Jean had no idea he was the Slasher and he asked Doyle if he could tell her himself, rather than having her read about it in the next day's paper. Twenty years later Doyle would tell *Mirror* reporter Frank Crook the story of what went on in the Scanlon house in the early hours on May 1, 1959.

"All right David," Doyle told him, "but when we get down there you tell her loud and bloody clear, because she is your wife. Speak up and give it to her."

So they took the short drive to Park Street in Arncliffe and knocked on the door of a house that is no longer there. Stirred from her slumber, Jean turned on the porch light and opened the door to see her husband flanked by two men.

"These men are the police, love," Scanlon told her, "They're detectives."

Scanlon then looked to Doyle as if hoping he would break the news, while Jean kept looking from one detective to the other. Doyle had to give Scanlon, a man who had no concern about hurting other women, a push to deliver the news that would surely hurt this one.

"Go on, David. You wanted to come down and see your wife. Tell her what's occurred."

"No, you do it," Scanlon begged.

"David, I told you at the station I would not tell your wife. This is a matter for you. Look, you're married to her. She's your wife, not mine."

His wife, standing on the porch in the middle of the night with no clue as what was going on, was getting sick of this.

"Will someone please tell me what's going on?"

Scanlon paused, took a breath, and said it quietly.

"I'm the Kingsgrove Slasher, love."

It was news that would devastate her, and would see her leave him two years later.

Night Terrors

It's hard not to feel a little sorry for the *Sydney Morning Herald* when it comes to coverage of the Slasher. The early hours of the Slasher attacks worked against the *Herald's* deadlines, and right into the hands of afternoon tabloids *The Mirror* and *The Sun*. While the Slasher's capture happened early enough for the morning broadsheet to get it on page one, it seems they didn't have the police contacts to confirm that it was actually the Slasher.

And so the paper ran with the dry headline "Man caught after chase". The story itself laid it on pretty thickly though; a reader would have to be an idiot not to realise the man they caught after the chase was the Kingsgrove Slasher. The police who caught him were described as "being members of a special patrol who have been keeping a close watch on the district". Those police were "hidden in nearby scrub, equipped with walkie-talkie wireless sets". The paper identified some of the police as coming from the elite 21 Division, which everyone knew had supplied the lion's share of the Slasher Patrol.

Both *The Sun* and *The Mirror* gave over their entire front page to the capture of the Kingsgrove Slasher. Oddly enough, *The Sun's* coverage never one mentions it *was* the Slasher; even the late edition mentions it was "a prowler" the police arrested. By 2pm, Scanlon had appeared in court and been named as the Slasher, so it's strange one of the afternoon tabloids appeared to drop the ball on what was the biggest story of the day.

It was *The Mirror* that managed to scoop them all. They had a photographer outside Kogarah police station to get *the* picture; Detective Sergeant Brian Doyle escorting a handcuffed David Scanlon from the back seat of an unmarked car. Doyle has his right hand firmly wrapped around Scanlon's forearm; even in a newsprint photo taken more than 50 years ago, it's easy to make out that his grip is so firm it has turned part of his hand white. There is no way this criminal is getting away. *The Mirror* did play it safe; they painted a white silhouette over everything but Scanlon's cuffed hands – just in case identifying the man would be a factor in any upcoming court case.

The very first word of the headline made it clear who was under that white silhouette – "Slasher caught, say police". *The Mirror's* coverage ran to two pages and dealt solely with Scanlon's court appearance. While he would eventually be charged with 18 attacks, that first visit to court saw him charged with the most violent – punching Lesley Coleman into unconsciousness, walloping Rosalie Meyer in the face with a block of wood and slicing open Marguerite Austin's abdomen with a razor.

The news of Scanlon's appearance in court led to the public cramming into the courthouse or waiting outside to catch a glimpse of the Slasher on the short perp walk from the police station next door. At least 50 people watched Doyle and Scanlon – on a break from long hours of questioning – walk to the courthouse, with press photographers' flashes going off. A photo captured what looked like Doyle gently holding Scanlon at the left wrist, though the cuffs that join the two are hidden by their jacket sleeves.

The cuffs would be removed when Scanlon entered the dock, where he sat chatting to police while waiting for the hearing to begin, and then clasped shut again five minutes later when his appearance was over. Wearing a white shirt open at the collar, a green sweater and a grey sports coat and trousers and sporting a face of dark stubble, he jumped to his feet when Magistrate EJ Etherton entered the court room. During the hearing Scanlon said just four words, all in response to questions from the magistrate.

Did he consent to the police request to keep him in Long Bay Jail until May 22?

"Yes, sir."

Did he wish to apply for bail?

"No, sir."

The police prosecutor, a Sergeant Boyd, did most of the talking during the five-minute hearing.

"Could it be noted that we allege that the defendant is the person who has been referred to very publicly as the Kingsgrove Slasher?" he asked, a question that would later cause some angst for Scanlon's court-appointed lawyer.

"The defendant was arrested at Turrella late last evening in dense scrub and had just some minutes previously been observed in two houses nearby.

"So far the defendant has been charged only with three matters but he has made more than 20 admissions of guilt and there will be a large number of other charges, all serious."

The magistrate agreed Scanlon should remain in jail to give police time to further investigate his crimes. With that, Scanlon was returned to the police interview room at the station next-door to continue answering questions.

33

*"I am going tell you that you are not obliged to speak or say anything at all or
answer any questions as anything you do say may be used in evidence."*
Brian Doyle's questioning of David Scanlon, May 1, 1959

As well as a break for a brief court appearance, some of
Scanlon's first day in custody was spent being taken around
to the various sites of his attacks, where he was asked to
identify the homes.

Visiting Walker Street, Turrella, he pointed to Marguerite
Austin's house through the car window and said "that is where I cut
the lady's stomach". He would identify the Colwell Street,
Kingsgrove home where Lesley Coleman was staying the night he
assaulted her by saying "this is the house where I punched the girl
in the mouth". While in Bayview Avenue, outside the home where
Rosalie Meyer lived in 1956, he said "That is the house where I hit
the girl with the piece of wood. That was one of the bad ones."

There was also time for a little supper, breakfast and lunch. But
the bulk of Scanlon's time on May 1, 1959, was spent sitting at a
table across from Detective Sergeant Doyle and explaining himself.
And as good a starting point as any was just why he did it all.

Doyle: What was your object in doing these things? What were you trying to prove?

Scanlon: It all started off quietly and innocently. I used to go out and have a bit of a look around. I suppose you would say that I started as a peeping Tom. I am a fast runner. I have run with St George Athletic Club. I can run the distance and I can sprint. I think that I have as much cunning as anyone else or as much as the average man … perhaps cunning is not the right word, I should say wits. I used to love using my speed and my wits to escape from people. I did all these things so people would chase me.

Scanlon claimed the thrill of the chase all started when he filled a paper bag with water and threw it at a man sitting in a car, with the view to getting him riled up enough for a pursuit. From that he said he went to flinging stones at passersby before deciding to do "some more serious things" so people would have a real reason to chase him.

Doyle didn't buy Scanlon's "chase" excuse. He noted that Scanlon was only chased once in 18 of his attacks and, as far as he could recall, never by the police.

Doyle: I am going to suggest to you that you got your thrills not from being chased but from creeping into bedrooms and deliberately inflicting cruelty on sleeping women.

Scanlon: No, it was the chase I enjoyed.

It's hard not to read that claim from Scanlon without heavy notes of denial. When Doyle further challenged Scanlon by pointing out that some of his victims – including children like seven-year-old Anne Willis or the bedridden Mona Sumner – were unlikely to chase him, Scanlon could do no more than just shrug his shoulders. The reality is that he was driven by the thrill of attacking sleeping women, though he seemed quite unable to admit to that.

The idea of the chase was something he created to avoid that reality; for a man apparently keen on being chased, he really had a habit of rushing out of his victims' bedrooms before an adult who could give chase arrived. Besides, if being chased was the point of the exercise, why did he wait until everyone was asleep before breaking into the houses?

Also, by his own admission, he crept into a lot of houses where he did nothing more than walk into the rooms and watch people sleep. People who had no idea he had ever been there. In those homes it seems the whole idea was to *avoid* being discovered and chased. And he had been into a *lot* of houses since 1956.

Doyle: Could you estimate the number of houses and backyards you have unlawfully entered since you have been doing this?

Scanlon: No, it would be terribly hard to say.

Doyle: Would it be hundreds or would it be thousands?

Scanlon: Many, many hundreds. perhaps thousands, I can't say. Sometimes I prowled around for as long as eight or nine hours.

Doyle: Would it be fair statement to say that you have been in most of the houses or yards in the vicinity of Marsh Street, Arncliffe, Walker Street, Turrella, and Banks Road, Earlwood?

Scanlon: Yes, that would be quite right to say that.

Later in the interview, Scanlon would add Eve Street (where he was almost captured in February) and Valda Avenue, Arncliffe (where his 17th victim Dale Batger lived), Highcliff Road in

Earlwood and where his family lived in New England Drive in Kingsgrove, to that list.

Scanlon told Doyle he didn't always carry a razor blade when he went prowling – he wasn't so armed on the night of his capture. When it came to the reason for cutting victims' bedsheets, clothing and occasionally the victims themselves, Scanlon again offered the sort of answer that suggested he was trying to hide the real truth of what he was doing – from himself as much as anyone else.

Doyle: I am suggesting to you that in some cases you didn't use the blade because you were disturbed in the rooms.
Scanlon: I didn't use the blade particularly to hurt the women but mainly to wake them up.
Doyle: How do you reconcile that with the fact that when some of them did wake up you further assaulted them?
Scanlon: Some of them will be hard to explain, I know.

Scanlon also told Doyle he had no intention of ever giving himself up – "I intended to go on and on" – then offered an odd explanation as to why.

Scanlon: My wife was the one I was worried about and she alone was one of the reasons why I would never give myself up.
Doyle: Do you think that your wife would have any knowledge of what you have been doing?
Scanlon: Not the slightest clue in the world. This will be a terrible shock to her. She is the one I have been worried about. I have simply told her in the mornings that I would be working back at night. She goes to bed fairly early and consequently she wouldn't know what time I got in. Other times when she would be getting

ready for bed I would tell her that I was going for a training run. I would put on my old sweater, a pair of trousers and rubber boots and off I would go. She would be sound asleep when I got home and she wouldn't know whether it was 11, 12 or 3 o'clock in the morning.

Doyle then questioned Scanlon on the specifics of each of his crimes, starting with the first three he would be charged with that day – Austin, Meyer and Coleman. He claimed to have been "jolted" when he read about the deep cut along the 64-year-old Austin's abdomen.

Scanlon: I couldn't understand it when I read that she got cut on the stomach because it was her breast I was trying to cut.
Doyle: Do you say that you cut her stomach in error and that you intended to give her that wound on the breast?
Scanlon: Yes, I thought I was cutting her higher up.
Doyle: I would have thought it would be difficult to inflict that injury to her stomach through all that clothing merely with a razor blade.
Scanlon: I don't say I did it in one strike of the blade. I had to move the blade up and down and cut through those things.

His explanation of the assault on 18-year-old Meyer was next, saying he repeatedly hit her with a block of wood because he "panicked".

Doyle: The girl received serious injuries and was kept in hospital for a couple of days. She had several stitches put in her forehead and she suffered concussions.
Scanlon: Yes, it is a pity that it turned out that way.

Doyle: You will appreciate the serious effects an event like this could have, not only on the body but on the mind of a girl of that age.

Scanlon: Yes.

Doyle: Why did you hit this girl on the head with a piece of 3x2 hardwood?

Scanlon: There is no answer to that one. I suppose I hit her because she woke up.

Then came the worst of his 18 attacks, the brutal assault on 21-year-old Lesley Jean Coleman, whom he punched so hard in the mouth that he broke her teeth, whom he punched so hard she lapsed into unconsciousness and almost choked on her own blood and teeth. Establishing what would be a trend in the questioning, Scanlon was open to explain the mechanics of the attack – how he got into the house, what weapon he used, what he did to the victim. But the reasons why he did what he did wasn't something Scanlon would give much consideration.

Doyle: Will you tell me why you assaulted this girl in this way?

Scanlon: I can only say that I wanted to wake her up.

Doyle: Following the assault the girl had to have a lot of medical and dental treatment. She had a series of X-rays taken of her mouth and jaw and had to receive treatment from an eye specialist for an injury to a tear duct received in the assault. She was very shocked and has suffered considerably with nerves since then. She has spent a lot of money on her recovery.

Scanlon: Yes, I suppose so.

His claim of "only wanting to wake her up" would also be used to explain the vicious gropings of 16-year-old Dale Batger and 14-year-old Helen Gaffey. Of the latter, he seemed to have fond memories of that night in February – "I remember it well. I was there for some time. I didn't cut the girl." ("but I didn't cut her" would be another weak excuse Scanlon would repeatedly offer during police questioning).

He took a similar inappropriate sense of joy in his cutting of Valerie Thompson while her husband lay beside her. "Yes, I did that. I remember it well. It amused me a good bit. She woke up and woke her husband up and he decided to chase me. That suited me … I got a lot of enjoyment out of it."

When Doyle pointed out the medical attention Valerie Thompson needed and that she has been "living in a state of fear", Scanlon seemed peeved at the intrusion on his special memories; "I suppose so."

Doyle would question Scanlon about the night he climbed up a ladder and into Georgina Palmer's North Shore bedroom. The serial criminal again showed interest in talking about how he did it but didn't want to spend much time thinking about what the attack had done to the 14-year-old Palmer.

Doyle: A ladder had been placed up to the girl's window, a towel had been taken from the windowsill and had been wrapped around the top of the ladder to use as a pad to deaden the noise of the ladder.

Scanlon: That is quite right. I brought the ladder in from next door. I used the towel to deaden the noise. I stood up on the ladder because the window was pretty high up.

Doyle: The cuts on the girl's breasts required medical attention.

Scanlon: Yes, I suppose so, although I don't think I cut her badly.

Doyle: Will you agree that such an assault on a young girl could have a far-reaching effect on [her] psychological make-up?

Scanlon: Yes.

He seemed similarly uninterested in pondering the effect his attack had on seven-year-old Anne Willis, merely answering "yes" to questions about her well-being. Elsewhere he tried to play down the severity, pointing out "I didn't cut the little girl". The only one of the 18 crimes that Scanlon wasn't questioned over was when he climbed into Marlene Storz's bedroom on the morning of July 4, 1956, where she was sleeping with her grandmother. That bout of questioning would happen in Long Bay jail four weeks later on May 28, when Doyle had the details of the incident.

Doyle: The girl's grandmother told me that when you got into the room she was in a sleepy stupor and that she thought you were her late husband coming back from the dead to see her. She reached her arms up and put them around your neck and said 'darling, now you have come back, never leave me again' and a moment later her granddaughter called to her that there was a man in the room.

Scanlon: I don't remember her doing that. As far as I can remember I went straight to the young girl's bed and cut the bedclothes. I am sure I would have remembered something like that.

Reading Doyle's court testimony (from which Scanlon's answers come) Scanlon comes across as a man in real denial. He's a man who doesn't want to admit – even to himself – the true motivation behind his crimes. To an outsider looking in, the sexual aspect is obvious, but Scanlon appeared desperate to frame his actions as a means to an end. It was all about the chase, he claimed. He didn't do these things because he got a thrill out of them but because they would lead to others pursuing him.

Scanlon was a man keen to avoid looking at his dark self within.

34

"I left my trade mark."
Daily Mirror headline, June 16, 1959

A week before Scanlon was questioned about the Storz home invasion, his case was back in court, and this time he had a barrister on his side – a K Kingston (none of the court reports record a first name for his legal representative). On May 22, Scanlon was back before Stipendiary Magistrate EJ Etherton, brought in a prison van from Long Bay and then led into court handcuffed to Detective Sergeant Doyle. The detective sat close to his prisoner, who occasionally blew on his hands to try and find some warmth in the chilly courtroom

Again, the courtroom was crowded with spectators – many of them women - who had come to see the Kingsgrove Slasher in the flesh. And it could have been the last chance they would have; Kingston was pushing to have the Scanlon trial held in a closed court "in the interests of justice".

Kingston's main – and perhaps only – argument was that his client had no chance of a fair trial as he had already been labelled as the Kingsgrove Slasher.

"Last time the matter was in court it was alleged by police that Scanlon was the Kingsgrove Slasher," Kingston told the court. "That received publicity in the papers. Should Scanlon in due course stand trial, I submit it would be virtually impossible for him to have a fair trial.

"He would go before the court virtually as the Kingsgrove Slasher, not as Scanlon."

It was a bit of a stretch, given the first person to say Scanlon was the Slasher was the man himself on the night he was arrested. That was something that didn't escape the attention of police prosecutor Sergeant Boyd.

"The defendant used the term referred to – we only followed suit," Sgt Boyd said.

Magistrate Etherton wasn't too keen on such a high-profile case going behind closed doors.

"I would be very loath to proceed in a court that was not open to the public," he said in deferring any decision until the start of Scanlon's committal hearing at Kogarah Local Court in June.

And his decision would be to have the hearings open to the public. That was great news for the afternoon papers, which would devote their front pages and four pages inside to blow-by-blow accounts.

The three-day committal hearing started on Tuesday, June 16. Scanlon was again represented by Kingston. Among the lawyer's recent cases was that of a nurse jailed for a year after firing a shot from a rifle at her ex-boyfriend. Denise Cox had broken things off with Graham Curry but he still owed her £120, so she made arrangements to meet and discuss that. For reasons that are unclear, she brought a rifle along, which she concealed under her topcoat.

When Curry looked away, she fired a shot. The judge accepted she wasn't trying to maim or kill him but felt that, unless he made an example of her, "he would be inviting every young woman in the community who had a grudge against a man to get a rifle and shoot at him," according to the *Sydney Morning Herald*.

At the prosecution table for Scanlon's hearing was police prosecutor Sergeant Rex Hamilton replacing Sgt Boyd. EJ Etherton was back in charge of the hearing, which wasn't a good thing for Scanlon if some of the magistrate's previous judgements were anything to go by. Etherton, who would retire in February of the following year, after 49 years in the legal profession, wasn't a soft-on-crime magistrate. In one case, he sent an unemployed 19-year-old labourer Kevin Brown to jail for stealing milk money home owners had left outside their front door for the milkman. "This type of theft is about as mean as one can imagine," Etherton said as he handed down his sentence.

Just a year before Scanlon's committal hearing, he jailed a 64-year-old pensioner for a month for lighting a fire during a fire ban. Clarence Watson had been burning the casing from copper wire so he could sell it to supplement his pension. The police prosecutor seemed to want the magistrate to go easy, pointing out there was no immediate danger and Watson had a water source nearby. However, despite Watson having no criminal record, Etherton sent him to the clink because "I feel I have to consider the matter in a very serious light; firstly as a punishment to yourself and secondly as a warning and deterrent to others".

So, it was unlikely Etherton was going to let someone like Scanlon off the hook.

When his hearing started, Scanlon faced charges over 18 attacks. They included grievous bodily harm, malicious wounding and breaking and entering (he was also charged over damaging a bedsheet owned by Noel Nicholls in 1956).

That morning, Scanlon – dressed in a double-breasted blue suit, yellow jumper and tie – was led to the dock in handcuffs. For the first few hours of the hearing, the gallery was crowded. The first witness to give evidence was Detective Sergeant Doyle, and he would take up most of the first day. At one stage police prosecutor Sgt Harrison would suggest the female members of the gallery leave, due to "the delicate nature" of the evidence. At that time, a female court stenographer was replaced by a man.

By today's standard the evidence was rather tame, though Etherton would apparently find it so shocking that, at the end of the hearing, he would seal the court transcript for 75 years.

Doyle related the bulk of the police questioning of Scanlon, going into detail about his offences. The police detective said he has asked why a number of the women had a "small cut on the breast". "He said 'It was just something to let them know the Kingsgrove Slasher had been in their rooms with them. It was sort of a trade mark I suppose. It was something to identify my jobs'."

Elsewhere Doyle said Scanlon denied he had any mental illness that drove him to do these things. "I said, 'have you ever suffered from blackouts, psychiatric disturbances or nerves?' He said 'no. I am in good health and condition. The only time I have been to a doctor is about eight or nine years ago when I had an infection in the middle ear. I got that at the Bankstown Baths'."

Doyle testified that Scanlon said he had not decided in advance which women to attack. "I just prowled about until I came across a suitable one," Doyle said Scanlon told him. "It is not as though I picked them out in advance, either the houses or the girls."

Surprisingly for a man who claimed he wanted to be chased, Doyle said Scanlon found all the media attention about the Slasher actually made it harder for him. "Publicity wasn't my object," Scanlon told him. "As a matter of fact the newspapers published more details than I would have wanted them to. They made people so Slasher-conscious that it was difficult for me to do anything."

Scanlon also made written statements about each of the 18 crimes. These were tendered to the court as exhibits in 1959 but remain subject to the 75-year restriction placed by Etherton (the trial transcripts were released as part of an appeal the author made in 2018).

Doyle finally finished his testimony in the mid-afternoon on the first day. He was followed by other police officers including constables Dallas Monley and Walter Gaffney, who were there on the night of Scanlon's arrest. Fingerprint experts Senior Constable Brefney Gorman and Sergeant Mervyn Wood testified about the prints found at the Gurney, Meyer, Palmer, Cousins and Gaffey homes.

The first victim to appear before the court was Rosalie Meyer, who was attacked at Undercliffe on the morning of November 26, 1956. Now 20 and working as a hairdresser, Meyer was still feeling the effects of that night in November – after her questioning she would leave the witness box in tears. In his questioning Sgt Harrison took her back to that night.

Q: Were you awakened about that time by something?
A: Yes.
Q: Are you aware or could you recollect what actually wakened you?
A: A throbbing head woke me up.
Q: When you wakened did you see anything?

A: I tried to but it was too dark.

Q: Did you hear anything?

A: Yes, I heard this noise, like the growling of a dog.

Q: Did you feel anything about that stage?

A: Yes, I was being attacked about the breasts.

Meyer told the court she screamed and the attacker fled moments before her mother and sister entered her bedroom. Until they saw the blood running down her face from being hit with a piece of wood, she said she was not aware of being struck with anything. Five stitches were inserted into the head wound, just below the hairline and she still bore the scar. Meyer added her knuckles were still affected from apparently trying to ward off the blows.

Q: How have you been since the attack?

A: For a long time I couldn't sleep on my own. I had to sleep in my father's room.

Q: How have you been recently?

A: For a year, I slept with the windows locked until I had bars on the windows, but now that we have bars I have been alright.

Her mother was also called to the stand, testifying that she didn't run to Rosalie's room as soon as she heard her daughter screaming, thinking she was just having a nightmare. She didn't make it to the bedroom before Rosalie stumbled out into the hall, blood dripping from a head wound. She identified the block of wood as being similar to the blood-stained one found inside her house that night. Sgt Harrison also questioned her about the mental state of her daughter.

Q: Did you notice anything else about her since the happening?

A: We put bars on the windows.

Q: Why did you do that?

A: Because she asked her father to. She couldn't sleep at night.

Q: Just a few minutes ago, when she went outside the court, was she a bit upset and hysterical?

A: She was crying, yes.

Q: Did she have any attacks of that kind after this attack?

A: When she used to read the papers about new attacks, she would get those crying attacks.

When it came to those papers, the way they covered Scanlon's trial showed the 1950s was a very different era. While the decade is remembered as a more straitlaced, conservative period, there was little thought given to protecting the privacy of victims of sex crimes – which is what Scanlon's assaults were. To modern eyes, the newspaper coverage of his trial seems quite invasive and insensitive. Eleven of his victims were under the age of 18 (and Meyer was aged 18); today that would likely see a judge slap a ban on the media publishing their names or anything else that would identify them. In 1959 there were no such obstacles for the media covering the Scanlon hearing. Names and photos of the victims – even the streets they lived on – were fair game.

The Mirror's coverage of the first day included a photo of Judith Gurney (aged 16 at the time Scanlon attacked her) on the front page. A photo of Lorraine Cousins (aged 17 when attacked) featured inside. Over the three days of the hearing, the tabloids would also run photos of underage victims Elaine Kelly, Gloria Geyson, Marlene Storz, Helen Downs and Anne Willis – the last was just seven years old at the time she woke to find Scanlon in her room.

The Mirror and *The Sun* would devote numerous full pages to covering the case in blow-by-blow detail. On the first day, *The Mirror* covered Doyle's testimony in such detail that it spread across four full pages and included the details of Scanlon's assaults on several of the underage victims. The tabloid also published the full addresses of 14 of the victims, including the youngest in Willis. Everyone in the city knew what the victims looked like, knew what had happened to them and, if they desired, could even visit them at home.

If someone committed the Slasher's crimes today, none of that would have appeared in the papers.

35

"She [Margaret Campbell] was suffering from 10 or 12 lacerations of the breasts apparently caused by a very sharp instrument."
The Sun reporting testimony from Dr Claire Burke, June 17, 1959

The Scanlon hearings were still a hot ticket with the public on the second day. A half-hour before the hearing was due to start at 10am, there was a queue of men and women at the front door of the courthouse. When the doors were thrown open at 9.50am, as many as 50 people rushed in to try and snare a seat in the public gallery. It was a case of musical courthouse chairs – not enough seats for the number of people, so those who missed out returned to the courthouse steps to watch the day's witnesses arrive in police cars.

Among the early arrivals were Marguerite Austin, a nurse at her side, and her daughter Valma Rogers (*The Sun*'s photographer snapped their pictures for the front page), followed by Mona Sumner and Eva Newstead, the mother of victim Lesley Coleman. Police ferried them through the gawkers outside the courthouse and into the witnesses' room, where they would wait for their turn to testify.

There was a chill in the courtroom itself, so before the proceedings got under way, a fire was lit in the fireplace to warm the room. At 10am, a handcuffed Scanlon was brought to the dock, dressed in the same clothes he had worn on the previous day. Once the defendant was in place, Magistrate Etherton started proceedings, with Austin called as the day's first witness. Sgt Hamilton didn't get off to the best start, asking her to confirm her full name was Marguerite May Austin, only to be told he had it wrong. "It is not 'May'," she said. "I don't know where the May came from".

He then took her through the events of November 19, 1958, when Scanlon leant into the bedroom window and hacked at her with a razor, slicing a deep gash along her abdomen.

Q: Was there much bleeding from this wound on the abdomen?

A: Yes, there was a terrible lot. By the time my daughter walked out of her room to my room, there was a pool of blood on the floor where I was standing. The police took the pajamas – they were all covered.

While her age and poor health were working against her before the attack, things had gone downhill since then. At several stages during Austin's testimony she had to rest, putting her hand to her head and closing her eyes. She told Sgt Hamilton what the assault had done to her health.

Q: Apart from the wound itself, did you suffer any after-effects as far as your nervous conditions is concerned?

A: Well, I haven't been well since. I have lost a stone in weight and I might tell you I only got up out of bed this morning to come here.

Q: We appreciate that. Would you tell his Worship whether this affair affected you as far as your nervous condition is concerned?

A: Oh well, it has affected me, but of course I suppose you couldn't expect anything else. I won't say it has made me frightened, because I am not the frightened kind, but I have slept with the window shut, a thing I never did in my life before.

Her daughter Valma Rogers followed her onto the stand, where her testimony supported that of her mother's – though she added that Austin stayed at her home until early in January 1959.

The order of the police case was to start with Scanlon's worst crimes; the bashing of Rosalie Meyer and the gashing of Marguerite Austin had been dealt with, which only left the assault on Lesley Coleman in the morning hours of July 14, 1956. Coleman herself would not appear in the court to give evidence; since 1956, she had married and moved to Western Australia. She did give a statement to Western Australian police, which was tendered to the court, but not released in 2018 along with the court transcript.

May Howell, who lived in the Colwell Street house where Coleman was attacked, did turn up to spend some time in the witness box. By this time, she had left Kingsgrove, moving to Auburn, perhaps to get away from the bad memories. Sgt Hamilton would ask her to dredge those up for the court.

Q: At about 4am on the 14th of July, 1956, were you awakened by something?

A: Yes, by my youngest son, he woke me up screaming.

Q: Your youngest son was screaming?

A: Yes.

Q: And did you go into Miss Coleman's room then?

A: Yes. My second youngest son [Kevin] and I ran towards the girl's room and saw her lying there, unconscious and covered with blood.

Q: And was the blood around her face, mouth and chest?

A: Yes, her face was badly gashed.

Howell testified that she and her son Kevin removed the teeth from Coleman's mouth so she didn't choke on them before regaining consciousness. She also told the court she saw a house brick covered with blood at the front door and there were also sprays of blood on the venetians in Coleman's room, on the wall behind her bed, and also in the room of her son who had woken screaming. She also noted that bedding in Kevin's room had been slashed – all of which suggested Scanlon had stayed in the house for some time after he battered Coleman.

After the attack, the family would continue to see Coleman when she came down for the dental work she needed.

Q: Did you notice she was very nervous?

A: Very nervous, she wouldn't stop in the house.

Q: Because of the nervousness?

A: Yes, she couldn't stay there again after that.

Coleman's mother Eva Newstead also testified, stating she was living at The Entrance at the time of the attack. Curiously, her testimony suggested she didn't see her daughter until two full days after the attack, when Coleman was driven up to her home. While Newstead had heard of the attack, this was the first time she had seen her daughter and the bruises and cuts on her body.

Q: Madam, did your daughter have any fits of unconsciousness or collapse whilst she was with you?

A: She was more or less under tablets that the doctor had given her and she used to lapse into sort of comas.

Newstead had noticed her daughter's behaviour had changed; she had gone from a "jolly type of girl" to one who dreaded the thought of being alone.

The last witness of the morning was Mona Sumner, Scanlon's second-last victim. The 72-year-old had been living with her son Norman's family in their Bardwell Park home – which backed onto the train line – when Scanlon stood at her window armed with a blunt penknife.

Q: At about 2.35am on the 11th February, 1959, were you wakened by something?

A: Yes, the cutting of the sheet and the hand. I saw the hand going out the window.

Q: Was it actually the grating noise of the cutting of the sheet [that] wakened you?

A: Yes.

When Sumner called out to Norman, his son Victor ran straight outside to see if he could catch Scanlon – but the villain had already fled across the train line and into the bush. Norman's daughter came into Sumner's room and noticed the cuts to her sheets and night dress. It was then, Sumner said, she noticed the blood coming from a cut to her left breast.

Q: How did this happening affect you?

A: Not just at the time but afterwards I sort of was upset.

Magistrate Etherton then called a short 15-minute adjournment; during that time, the people in the packed public gallery sat tight. No one wanted to give up their seat with others waiting outside for a chance to sit and watch the proceedings.

After the adjournment, Dale Batger took the stand. In January that year, the 16-year-old had been groped so forcefully by Scanlon that he held on even after she rolled away on her bed, pulling him through the window and into her room. Sgt Hamilton had the difficult task of walking Batger through that night, and she seemed quite uncomfortable about some of the questioning.

Q: What do you feel?
A: A man squeezing me.
Q: Whereabouts?
A: On the breasts.
Q: And was it a gentle squeeze, or medium, or hard?
A: Hard.
Q: Did it cause you any pain?
A: Yes.
Q: What kind of pain?
A: Sharp pain, I expect.
Q: Sharp pain?
A: Oh yes, I suppose so.

For some reason, a few minutes later Sgt Hamilton would return to the groping, again asking her what it felt like and how she would describe the pain. Batger would testify that her breasts went very dark with bruising and later began to peel. She also said at no stage did she see the man who had done it.

Night Terrors

For the first time that day, Scanlon's barrister decided to cross-examine a victim (he had briefly questioned Rosalie Meyer the previous day). As would be the case throughout the three-day hearing, Kingston's questions seemed odd; they didn't appear to highlight anything that might suggest his client's innocence or even throw up any mitigating circumstances. Looking at his five questions to Batger, it was hard to understand his strategy.

Q: Were you going to work at the time this happened?
A: Yes
Q: Did you go to work the following day?
A: Yes.
Q: And have you been to work every day since?
A: Yes.
Q: You are sleeping alright?
A: Oh, yes.
Q: Have there been many nights since then when you have not slept well?
A: Yes.

In summary, Batger went back to work and sometimes doesn't sleep well. Hardly the sort of thing likely to get a client off the hook. The testimony of her mother Joan, who took the stand next, made things worse for Kingston and his client. She was the first to provide vivid evidence of the ongoing mental trauma inflicted by one of Scanlon's attacks.

Early in her testimony, Joan said that when she rushed to Batger's bedroom she found her daughter on the floor screaming with her hands covering her face. There would be an echo of that behaviour in how she described her daughter since the attack.

Q: Have you noticed anything about her behaviour since this incident?

A: Yes, she is very, very nervy. She won't be left alone.

Q: And have you noticed her doing anything unusual since this happening?

A: Yes.

Q: What it is?

A: Hiding behind chairs, the lounge chairs and the lounge, and she won't go outside to the toilet, even in daylight.

Q: And on these occasions that she has been hiding herself behind the lounge chairs, what was she doing when you discovered her?

A: Mostly hiding her face, hiding her fear.

Joan said the other children in the house had also been upset since the assault and she had been calling in Detective Sergeant Doyle to come to the house and allay their fears; his most recent visit had been in April, a month before Scanlon's arrest.

Kingston chose to cross-examine Batger's mother, though some clumsy questioning allowed her to further highlight the depth of her daughter's fears.

Q: Dale's behaviour is quite normal now, isn't it?

A: No, not quite.

Q: Well in what way…

A: She is still very nervy.

Q: What does she do that is not normal?

A: She doesn't like to be in a room on her own. She won't enter any room on her own and she won't go out.

Q: She is not going out at night?

A: Not unless there is some company right from the door.

On the morning after the attack, Batger's mother took her to Rockdale doctor Jack Lofberg. He was called to the stand to describe the bruising Batger had suffered. He told Sgt Hamilton there was "clear thumb and finger bruises" visible around both breasts; the thumb marks at the top and fingers below. He concluded they could only have been left by someone standing behind her at the time.

Q: From your examination could you say whether any great pressure had been applied by the fingers and thumbs?
A: I couldn't say exactly. That part would bruise easily, but considerable pressure must have been applied.

Of all the victims, it would be his last who proved the most resilient. Fourteen-year-old Helen Gaffey was groped by Scanlon in a similar fashion to Batger, after he had taken numerous items of clothing from her room to the backyard where he tore them with his bare hands. She was asked by the police prosecutor how she felt in the days after the February attack. She replied that it took her a little while to get over it. "After then I was quite alright", adding that she slept soundly in her own bed the night after the attack.

Not really getting the answer he wanted, Sgt Hamilton pressed on in an apparent effort to get the schoolgirl to admit some ongoing mental trauma. But Gaffey wouldn't play ball.

Q: Have you any idea how long it took you to get over it, Helen?
A: Oh, I think about a fortnight.
Q: How did you feel during that fortnight, were you able to sleep in that room?
A: Oh, I was able to sleep.

Q: In the same room?

A: That is right.

Q: How did you feel about going out on your own at night time?

A: I didn't like going out very much on my own for a while at night.

Q: Do you have an outside toilet at your place?

A: Yes.

Q: How did you feel about going down there?

A: For a couple of nights I didn't like going out there by myself, but after then I was quite okay.

Sgt Hamilton had better luck with Gaffey's mother Mary, who admitted her daughter's behaviour had changed since the attack. She said her daughter wasn't the same girl she was before. "Helen never at all at any time before this was nervous," she said. "She would stay in the house and look after the kiddies if I wanted it and she was never frightened to go to the toilet, but I am afraid, since then, we have not been able to leave her and she generally likes company when she goes to the toilet."

Q: Were other members of the family affected by this experience, Mrs Gaffey?

A: I am afraid my husband never slept for about two months after. He was about the worst of the lot, and one other little boy, who had asthma. He was pretty jittery, on edge for quite a while.

The last witness to give evidence before the court adjourned for lunch was Elaine Kelly. Wearing cat's eye spectacles and a twinset, the 17-year-old secretary said she remembered being woken by the sound of heavy breathing and the bedsheets being pulled across her body.

Q: Did you look around shortly after that to see if there was anything happening?

A: No. I just laid real quiet and just listened.

Q: Did you hear anything further?

A: No, I just turned around quick and started to scream like anything.

Q: When you started to scream did you see anything?

A: Well, what I saw was a foot going out the window, a pair of feet just dived straight out the window.

She also spoke of finding a wet bra on the bedroom floor that didn't belong to her, and of not noticing the cuts to her bedsheet until she came home from work the following day and not spotting the scalpel blade Scanlon had left in her bed. Even though Scanlon had not cut her at all, she told Sgt Harrison she had been taking sleeping tablets of an evening.

Q: Elaine, did you cry easily before this happening?

A: Not before.

Q: Have you cried since the happening?

A: Yes.

Q: On many occasions?

A: Yes.

Q: And have you had any signs of trembling or anything like that?

A: Yes.

Q: How long has that persisted for?

A: I still get it now.

Q: Are you able to move about alone at night time?

A: No.

After Kelly's evidence, the court took a recess. By the time it returned later that afternoon, the local high school students had finished their lessons for the day. Some of them were as intrigued as their parents about the Kingsgrove Slasher case and so headed to the courthouse. Teenaged schoolgirls, still in their uniforms, began milling about outside the court watching witnesses arrive. Keen to try and catch a piece of the proceedings, some of them moved into the building and stood close to the courtroom doors to see if they could hear any of the goings-on. Later, as adults began to leave the public gallery, some students managed to find a seat in the courtroom itself, getting to see what the Slasher looked like for themselves and to hear what he had done to some of his victims.

The first victim they would have heard from was Valerie Thompson, who was attacked while her husband lay in bed next to her and their baby was asleep in a bassinet just outside their bedroom door. She said she woke just after midnight on October 29, 1956 and saw the dark shadow of a man leaning over the bed. She called out to her husband and, at that, Scanlon fled the bedroom, almost knocking over the bassinet in the hall. Her husband Ron gave chase but could not catch Scanlon.

Georgina Palmer was called to the stand. Now a 17-year-old receptionist, she was just 14 when Scanlon walked down the road from the Lavender Bay guest house where he lived with his new wife and tried to get into her room. She told the court what happened on that night, breaking down when she spoke about seeing Scanlon standing on the ladder he'd placed against the wall under her bedroom window.

"Calm yourself, Miss Palmer," Sgt Hamilton said. "There is no need to get upset, just take it quietly. Would you like a glass of water or something?"

Palmer nodded and a police officer brought her a glass. She took a shaky sip and smiled to the officer before gathering herself and continuing her testimony.

Q: Was it when you saw this man on the ladder that you called out for your parents?
A: That's right.
Q: How did you call out, loudly?
A: Fairly loudly, yes.
Q: Could you say whether the man was right outside the window or …
A: Yes.
Q: What did you shout out - do you remember?
A: I think it was "Mummy, there's someone in the room".

After her parents ran into the room, Palmer said they noticed her bloodstained pajama top and then the cuts to her chest Scanlon had inflicted.

The only victim not to have been attacked while in a house was up next. Margaret Campbell was quizzed by Sgt Hamilton about that night in March 1956 when she and a "male friend" had parked in scrub at Beverly Hills. She recalled it was a hot night and the car doors had been left open to let in whatever breeze there may have been.

Q: And you remained there for some little time and did you eventually notice a stinging sensation in your breasts?
A: Yes, I did.
Q: Did you then immediately notice that the yellow frock you were wearing had been cut in several places in line with your breasts?
A: Yes.

179

Q: And there was about a dozen cuts in all?
A: Yes, 12 cuts.
Q: And were they all on the breasts, except one which was in the direction of your armpit?
A: Yes.
Q: Was there much bleeding, Miss Campbell?
A: Yes, at the time it happened.
Q: Do you still have scars on the breasts from those cuts?
A: Yes, I have got three scars.

Allan Lauchlan, director of AW Kemp, the company Scanlon worked for, would also testify that day, largely to explain where the accused got the scalpel blade he used on Elaine Kelly. Lorraine Cousins, who was asleep the entire time Scanlon was in her room slashing clothing, took the stand, while a statement from Annette Gurney (who had since moved to Queensland with her family) was tendered to the court as the hearing wound down for the day.

36

"The small court was packed throughout yesterday's short hearing, with spectators standing at both doors."
Sydney Morning Herald, June 19, 1959

O
n the last day of the hearing interest in the case was still high, with people queuing up outside the courthouse waiting for the doors to open. On that Thursday morning Scanlon had been brought from Long Bay Jail to the court more than an hour early. He would pass that hour in the exercise yard adjoining the cells at the nearby Kogarah police station. Someone handed him an electric razor so he could shave before he headed over to the court.

Testimony on the final day would include Scanlon's youngest victims; Anne Willis and Marlene Storz aged seven and 12 respectively when he crept into their rooms. Also, the only person to strike a blow against Scanlon would appear – 19-year-old Elaine Eardley.

One of the other victims to testify on the last day was Gloria Geyson. The black and white photos show Geyson as a bottle blond with wavy hair a round face and dark eyebrows, she was just 12 years of age when she woke and found Scanlon in her room trying to pull away her blankets.

Q: Were you awakened and did you see anything or anybody?

A: Well, I was in a deep sleep and I woke up and I thought it might have been my mother tugging the bed clothes and when the tugging kept on I turned around and saw the shape of a man. I thought it must have been my father so I just said "Dad" and I put my hand up to his face and then he went to put my thumb in his mouth. I started to yell out to mum.

Q: And how did you yell out?

A: I didn't scream, I wasn't sure.

Q: You were still not quite sure?

A: No, I just said "Mum" a few times.

That was when she realised it was an intruder because he ran out of her room, leaving her with cuts across her pajamas and chest.

Q: Did you go back to your bedroom for the next few nights or what?

A: No I think I slept with my mother and father.

Q: Did you eventually go back to your own room?

A: Oh yes but sometimes I kept on going into mum's room and I felt rather scared, you know.

Q: How long did this nervousness continue?

A: Well it was when all the, when the slashing was still going on. I was still nervous and when it all finished I was alright most of the time, then when it started again I got nervous again.

Q: And when you read of the arrest of a certain person, did the nervousness disappear?

A: Yes.

Night Terrors

Scanlon's barrister cross-examined Geyson and, if his aim was to show she was now unaffected, it backfired.

Q: You are quite alright now?
A: Yes.
Q: And when did you last sleep in your mother's room?
A: I have been sleeping in the lounge room a couple of times when I was scared.
Q: In the lounge room, when was that?
A: Friday night.
Q: Last Friday night?
A: Yes
Q: What made you scared?
A: I went up to my girlfriend's. I saw this man in a laneway and I just got scared after that.

Before Anne Willis could give her testimony, Magistrate Etherton ran her through a series of questions to gauge whether the now 10-year-old understood she had to tell the truth.

Q: If you take the Bible in your right hand and you promise to tell the truth, the whole truth and nothing but the truth and ask God to help you and you tell a lie, do you know what would happen to you?
A: Yes
Q: What would happen to you?
A: Something would happen to you that would be nasty or something would go wrong and it wouldn't be so good.
Q: Can you say more exactly what might happen to you?
A: You just get some sort of a punishment.

Q: By whom?
A: God.

At that, Magistrate Etherton decided the girl could testify. It would only be Sgt Hamilton who questioned Willis; the defence barrister Kingston would rightly see little benefit in trying to poke holes in a 10-year-old's testimony. The police prosecutor took her back to that night in July 1956.

Q: Do you remember what caused you to wake up, Anne?
A: Yes
Q: What did you feel?
A: A man was cutting all of my clothes, my bed clothes.
Q: And you indicated at the front here that was in around your chest?
A: All my pajamas were cut and everything.
Q: Do you remember what you did when this happened?
A: Yes, I called out to my father and he wouldn't believe me and he just told me to go back to sleep.

She said that, after she called out, she saw the figure of the man walking out of her bedroom door and into the hallway. Willis called out again for her mum and dad; this time they came and saw their daughter's slashed blanket and pajamas. Three years had passed since the attack, and Willis said she had only just returned to sleeping in that room.

Her mother Marjory was next onto the stand and told the court all the doors were locked on that night, with only two windows open – one in their room and another in the bathroom. Scanlon would climb through the bathroom window, removing a flyscreen in a frame. Marjory still remembered hearing her daughter call out in the darkness.

Q: How did she call out?

A: She screamed out "Daddy, there's a man in my room" and we thought she was having a nightmare and my husband said "You're alright pet. Go back to sleep" and a few minutes later she screamed out again.

Q: You realised there was something wrong and jumped up?

A: Yes.

Q: You went to Anne's room?

A: My husband got up and brought her into bed with me.

Q: And how was she?

A: She was very upset, of course. She was crying.

Marjory also told the court that, after the police had left, they discovered the blankets in their own bedroom had also been slashed. Kingston was more willing to confront Marjory on the details of her testimony, both through cross-examination and objecting during the police prosecutor's questioning. In both cases it's hard to see what he was trying to do, as his actions only served to allow for more damaging statements from Willis' mother.

Kingston raised an objection to her claim that they had been having "a terrible time with [Anne]" since the attack. That prompted Sgt Hamilton to ask for detail so as to clarify what she meant. "I could say just about every night for two years we have put her in her own bed for an hour or two hours," she said. "She woke up screaming so we had a stretcher in our room all the time and when she would waken we would bring her straight into our room and she would spend the night there." As well as the family doctor, Marjory took her daughter to see a child specialist and also a psychiatrist.

Q: And how is Anne progressing as a result of all this consultation, can you tell me?

A: Well, at the moment she is better than she has been since it happened but up to this [point] we have had to treat her very carefully and consider her in every way. She still wouldn't go into the bathroom by herself unless somebody goes in before her.

In cross-examination, Kingston got her to repeat testimony about Willis sleeping with her parents for two years after the attack and asked her about the medical visits – which introduced testimony about how a girl who was just seven at the time was prescribed sedatives to help her sleep. His questioning also brought up Willis' fear of the dark, which had only surfaced since 1956.

Q: You say she occasionally shows a fear of the dark now?

A: Yes.

Q: In what way does she show it?

A: Well we have a manhole in our bathroom. She is terrified that someone might come through the roof in the bathroom. She will never go in the bath by herself unless someone goes in first to look behind the shower recess. And she never goes outside the back door at night by herself.

If Kingston's strategy was to try and diminish the seriousness of Scanlon's attack on a seven-year-old girl, it did not appear to have worked. If anything it made the girl's experience seem *more* terrifying.

Night Terrors

After a short adjournment, the court would hear about the only one of the 18 charges Scanlon faced where the victim was not human. On August 14, 1956, Dora Nicholls had woken to the sound of blinds flapping against the window in the bedroom where her 12-month-old daughter Kim was sleeping. Her husband Noel testified that he went into the room and found the pillow and bedspread on the spare bed had been slashed.

Q: There was no person sleeping in that particular bed, your infant daughter being in a bed on the other side of the room?

A: My wife had slept there for about half an hour in between, about 12 o'clock. My daughter had woken up during the night and she wouldn't go back to sleep and my wife had been there for about half an hour about 12 o'clock.

In press photographs of Marlene Storz arriving at the court, the 14-year-old looks like a very serious young girl. She wore horn-rimmed glasses, short hair in a ponytail and a slightly stern look on her face. The night of Scanlon's visit in July 1956, Marlene was asleep in the room she shared with her grandmother Emma Wurst, the two beds separated by a partition. She said that, at about 5am, she was woken by something pushing at her back.

Q: When you woke up did you see anybody?

A: I saw a dark shadow rushing [to] the foot of my bed and it stayed there.

Q: Did you speak?

A: Yes.

Q: What did you say?

A: My brother's name because I thought it was him.

Q: You spoke, using the German language, and saying "Is that you, Hans?"

A: Yes.

Q: And did this person make any reply?

A: He … he just jumped out the window.

The final witnesses at Scanlon's committal hearing related to his 15th attack, at Duff Street, Arncliffe. It was an early morning attack, where a teenager and her two younger nieces were asleep. The nieces were Helen and Sharon Downs and the teenaged aunt was Elaine Eardley, whose actions would make the front page of that afternoon's edition of *The Sun*.

Helen slept through the assault, which involved Scanlon running his hand along the-then 11-year-old girl's body and groping her breasts, so she could not really provide too much information. But something had woken up Eardley and she caught Scanlon in the act, reaching through the window over her niece's bed.

Q: What was this person doing?

A: When I woke up I saw a hand through the venetians. They weren't quite down at all and the venetians were out slightly and I just saw the hand in and it did look as if it had been on the young lass' body. It was in that same area.

Q: Did you see the hand actually touch the body of the girl at any stage?

A: Well, no, I can't say I did then. All I could say is I think … I am not sure.

Q: What did you do?

A: I picked up a shoe, a high-heeled shoe, and I slipped out of bed.

Q: One of your high-heeled shoes?

A: Yes, I slipped out of the bed across the room, jumped on the bed, pulled the venetians out and then I hit him with the shoe.

Q: And how did he appear to respond to that?

A: He went back when I hit him. He went back, stood back and seemed to be stunned … Well, he was … he just didn't expect it.

Q: Can you remember what you said?

A: Oh, I smashed the window first and that's when I called out "Go on, get out", I think.

Eardley said Downs was left with several red marks on her skin, including on her breast and down her side.

Q: Did that little girl appear disturbed over this incident?

A: Yes.

Q: She woke up?

A: When I got up on the bed I trod on her leg and that disturbed her.

When Kingston chose not to cross-examine, it brought the parade of witnesses to an end. If those in the public gallery had hoped to see Scanlon take the stand, hear the man explain in his own voice just why he did it, they would be sorely disappointed. Scanlon would be a largely mute figure in the courtroom, saying only a few words.

With Scanlon staying in the dock guarded by police detectives it was time for Magistrate Etherton to decide whether he had to stand trial or if he could walk free without a case to answer.

After a short adjournment, the public gallery was full after the news a decision was in the offing. Those able to snare a seat in the courtroom heard Scanlon's barrister challenge seven of the 18 charges, saying the Crown had not established a prima facie case.

This included the attack on 16-year-old Dale Batger, where Scanlon was charged with inflicting grievous bodily harm. Kingston said Batger was only groped by Scanlon which he claimed fell short of the serious nature of the charge.

"I submit it would be absurd to regard an injury of this nature which cleared up in three weeks as amounting to grievous bodily harm," he said to the magistrate.

He added any mental injury – such as shock – had only been of a temporary nature. Prosecutor Sgt Hamilton referred to a previous case of a man charged with rape and assault where the judge said "There was a time when shock was not regarded as bodily hurt but the day has gone by when that could be said".

The prosecutor said it would be wrong to "cast aside" all of Batger's reactions. "In this case an intruder in the small hours of the morning entered this girl's room by placing his hands through the window and gripping this girl very strenuously, exercised pressure on both her breasts," Sgt Hamilton said.

"Your worship can well imagine the agonising terror endured by a girl in such circumstances."

Indeed he could, for Magistrate Etherton found Scanlon had a case to answer on the Batger charge.

Kingston took the same approach with what Scanlon had done to his final victim Helen Gaffey. "I would submit that, having seen her in the box and having heard the medical evidence, you would be of the opinion that she is now a normal person," he said.

The magistrate again wasn't interested and set the Gaffey charge for trial as well. It was the same for the Valerie Thompson charge, despite Kingston's efforts to point out she only suffered a little cut that didn't really cause her any problems. With the case of Georgina Palmer, he said Scanlon had ample time to do whatever he wanted to her but only cut her breasts. That apparent discretion from

Scanlon argued against a grievous bodily harm charge. A similar argument was mounted to downgrade the attack on Gloria Geyson

For Kelly, Kingston said the fact she had continued to sleep in the same room pointed to any shock she suffered not being of the grievous kind.

Magistrate Etherton wasn't having a bar of it and found Scanlon would have to answer all those charges at trial. He did throw Kingston a bone; he removed the "break" from the "break and enter" charge relating to the Annette Gurney case, ruling the prosecution hadn't provided any evidence of breaking in.

After a short adjournment, the magistrate would read out the 18 charges – a process which would take seven minutes. During that time, Scanlon remained standing with his hands clasped in front of him. After committing him to trial, Magistrate Etherton asked if Scanlon had anything to say. In a soft voice, he said what was likely his only words at the hearing; "On the advice of my counsel, Your Honour, I have nothing to say".

Bail was not asked for and then formally refused, with Scanlon taken back to the cells until at least August 24 – when his case would go to trial.

37

"... it became fashionable for women to allege they had been attacked by the Kingsgrove Slasher ..."
Trial testimony of Detective Sergeant Brian Doyle, September 7, 1959

As it turned out Scanlon would have to wait a little longer for his day in court. He didn't appear before Sydney's Central Criminal Court until Monday, September 7. Presiding over the trial was Justice Bruce Macfarlan; Scanlon's trial was his first since being appointed to the NSW Supreme Court in late July. Representing Scanlon was QC Simon Isaacs, who had recovered from a car accident he and his wife had been involved in earlier that year.

Isaacs' name regularly appeared in newspaper court reports. In June 1956, he represented Donald Robertson, described by the *Sydney Morning Herald* as "a 19-year-old cripple". He had been charged with the murder of a 77-year-old shopkeeper, whom he repeatedly hit on the skull with a hammer. Arguing that his client's "mentality was subnormal" and he couldn't form the intention to kill, Isaacs saw the sentence reduced to manslaughter. Nicolson was sentenced to 10 years ("Cripple sent to gaol", the *Herald*'s somewhat insensitive headline read the next day).

Isaacs wouldn't be so successful in reducing a sentence later that same year. In September his client William Parson would be found guilty of murdering Pearl Lyons during a lovers' quarrel. Three months later, a bogus doctor client of Isaacs would manage to commit suicide in the court cells two hours after being sentenced to eight years for manslaughter.

John Niven was an illegal abortionist and, in December, he was found guilty of the manslaughter of Florence Maloney, who died at his Paddington home after a botched abortion. Pleading leniency, Isaacs said it was likely she had died from shock brought on by an overuse of anaesthetic, which was accidental.

Found guilty, Niven was taken to the courtroom cells to be transported to Long Bay jail. He was sharing the cell with several other men, who watched as he pulled a bottle with some white pills from his pocket and swallowed them with a glass of water. "Don't touch me," he warned the other prisoners. "I have taken strychnine. I am a doctor. I will be dead in five minutes … I am starting to go. Soon it will all be over."

He then slumped to the floor, writhing in agony as the prisoners called for the police. Niven was taken to St Vincent's Hospital but died 10 minutes after his arrival. Police officers suggested Niven had hidden the pills in his cell before appearing in court.

On the opening day of Scanlon's trial the court's gallery was "crowded" (if you read *The Mirror*) or "almost empty" (if you picked up *The Sun* of an afternoon). If there was anyone in that gallery of the morning of September 7, 1959, they would have heard Scanlon say just one word, but say it 18 times over. As Justice Macfarlan read out each charge, Scanlon – dressed in a navy suit, white shirt and a woolen tie – uttered the word "guilty". The process took almost 10 minutes, but the afternoon tabloids already had their front-page headlines – *The Mirror*'s fronter would scream "Slasher guilty!" while *The Sun* went for "The Slasher" in a huge black typeface and "pleads guilty to 18 charges". Despite the guilty pleas, there would still be enough going in the day's trial for *The Sun* to fill two full pages and for *The Mirror* to splash it over four.

Once the charges were read and Scanlon's pleas entered, Crown prosecutor WJ Knight QC noted the prisoner had no criminal record, before bringing Detective Sergeant Doyle to the stand. His testimony would fill 11 tightly-typed foolscap pages of the trial transcript and include a description of all 18 crimes as well as detailing Scanlon's background. That painted a picture very much at odds with most people's assumptions of the depraved character someone like the Kingsgrove Slasher must have possessed.

"The prisoner does not drink and is not an associate of criminals, prostitutes or undesirables," Doyle said. "He bore an excellent character prior to his arrest and was very highly regarded by his employers. As far as I can ascertain he was well liked by everyone who knew him."

He told the court of the night in 1951 when, aged 22, Scanlon arrived home at New England Drive, Kingsgrove, and tripped over the body of his dead mother lying on the floor. "His father later remarried. The prisoner has got on very well with his stepmother and both he and she have told me that they have the highest regard for each other." The effect of Scanlon discovering his mother's body and subsequent relationships with women would be brought up later in the trial by psychiatrist testifying for the defence.

Doyle would describe the police hunt for the Slasher, claiming his crimes "are absolutely without precedent in this country and I can find no record of any exact parallel overseas".

"The crimes committed by him have had a seriously adverse effect over a long period of time on the lives of perhaps hundreds of thousands of people living in the areas raided by him. Such effects will not quickly be removed. A good number of the entire population of the districts were living in constant fear and apprehension that their house may well be the next to be raided by the prisoner."

Doyle saw fit to explain the newspapers had, over the years of the Slasher's raids, blamed him for crimes he never committed. Those were either committed by a copycat or were faked by the "nervous and neurotic" victims themselves. "I am satisfied he has been charged with and pleaded guilty to every serious crime committed by him. There are no other outstanding serious crimes to be proffered against him, nor is he suspected of any further serious crimes."

There were, Doyle admitted, some minor matters Scanlon had not been charged with, including malicious damage "to brassieres and back verandahs and that sort of thing", where the value of the damaged goods was less than £1.

During the long hours Doyle sat across from Scanlon during the police interviews, he said he found the man willing to "put his cards on the table" and admit to exactly what he had done. But Doyle felt that wasn't out of a sense of guilt. "He showed no contrition that I could detect. His main contrition seemed to be for the fact that he was captured. On the other hand I did perceive an air of smug satisfaction in his replies to some questions."

He then gave Justice Macfarlan an overview of each of Scanlon's 18 raids, much of which summarised the evidence Doyle had already given at the committal hearing. He'd not gotten through the first one, that of Lesley Coleman, before the Justice intervened to ask if Doyle's interrogation had touched on why Scanlon so often injured the women's breasts. "I think he said words to the effect that it was his trade mark, 'it was something to identify my jobs, that was something to let them know the Kingsgrove Slasher had been with them', and when they had other injuries that was a fact, they also had a nick on the breast."

Doyle spoke of the four days Rosalie Meyer spent in hospital after Scanlon hit her in the face with a block of wood, of the amusement the prisoner took in talking about slashing Margaret Campbell while she sat in a car with a boyfriend, the ongoing problems suffered by the youngest Slasher victim Anne Willis, that he lent in to slash the sheets on an empty bed in the Nicholls' house to keep the police hunt going, how he prowled in torrential rain before raiding Elaine Kelly's house and then ran the three kilometres back to his own home.

There appeared to be no rhyme or reason as to how he chose the houses to raid. "I am quite satisfied in no case did the accused select a victim in advance," Doyle said, "but he prowled about until he came across a suitable bedroom. On some occasions he may have prowled around for hours and hours before he eventually stopped at a suitable place. One night he prowled from about 9pm until 5.15am."

Under cross-examination from Isaacs, Doyle said there was no evidence Scanlon had raped any of his victims. Isaacs also questioned Doyle on whether Scanlon had spoken about getting a "thrill" out of being chased by police, which had been the excuse the prisoner offered to explain his actions.

Doyle was the only prosecution witness and, after he left the stand, the Crown rested. With Scanlon pleading guilty, all that was left for his barrister was to look to offer a defence of diminished responsibility, that he was not in his right mind when he committed the crimes. For that the defence would rely on a psychiatrist and a psychologist. The former was Dr Ignacy Listwan, who interviewed Scanlon twice in May at Long Bay (he had previously seen one of Scanlon's sisters as a private patient). Isaacs had an odd style of questioning his witnesses; he would start a question by saying "you were told …", leaving his witness nothing more to do than say "yes" in reply.

One such question, that provided detail of Scanlon's relationship with his wife Jean, was more than 500 words long. In that question – to which Dr Listwan literally answered with one word, "Yes" – Isaacs said Jean felt Scanlon was a "very good husband".

"The routine was," Isaacs' question continued, "he came home around 6.15pm and at 7pm after dinner they were sitting in the lounge, he usually reading the paper and listening to the serials and she knitting". In the months preceding Scanlon's capture, that had changed because he told her he had to work overtime. But if she asked him to come home earlier, he would. Jean never thought to check with his employer about the overtime; Scanlon gave her his pay-packet and there was always an extra few pounds to cover that extra work.

"She told you their sex relations were normal in frequency and type and he was satisfied with his emotional outlets … The prisoner's wife describes him as a quiet man. He was very good to her but she could not get through to him. She used to get cranky with him but would never have an argument because of his retiring nature."

Scanlon was a neat man, Isaacs 'asked' Dr Listwan in that 500-word question, who would "criticise" Jean if she left a pair of shoes out. He was also a runner and had, at one stage held the St George District Amateur Athletics Club's running records in six different distances – from 75 yards (68 metres) to 10 miles (16 kilometres).

Scanlon would tell Dr Listwan that he had a sheltered upbringing and felt closer to his mother than his father, who was stricter. The doctor felt Scanlon's relationship with his mother led to his being in a "state of sexual immaturity". Then "when his mother died in 1951 that was the starting point where he came out of balance," Dr Listwan said. "Other women appeared in his life and there was his step-mother who also played a great part as a substitute for his mother. Then he married in 1956 and I think with a great amount of apprehension and again it was a sort of a mother figure for him." Listwan felt it no coincidence that his "abnormal behaviour" commenced around the time his step-mother and Jean came on the scene.

On his crimes, Scanlon told the doctor they arose out of a "build-up of nervous tension" which led him to act in a way he could not control. Dr Listwan agreed with Detective Doyle's statements that Scanlon's crimes were rare, saying he could only find three similar cases in the literature. These were a physician who, when drunk, could only ejaculate after pricking his partner and seeing blood flow, a soldier who would attack women by stabbing them in the genitals and a man who would stab women in the arm with a dagger, causing himself to ejaculate.

The doctor's diagnosis would be that Scanlon was "a sex-perverted psycho-neurotic". He suffered from a kind of obsessive-compulsive "psycho-neurosis", where the compulsive side ruled and forced him to carry out actions against his wishes. "Any compulsive acts are usually done in a subconscious urge to do them, which the prisoner could not resist," the doctor told the court. "It is not controlled by our willpower and therefore the responsibility is diminished."

There were also sadistic tendencies but, curiously, the doctor claimed Scanlon got a greater thrill from being chased. While it was something he would never be cured of, Dr Listwan said treatment would help him successfully control those impulses. What also would help was that Scanlon's inflated "feeling of a master mind" due to his ability to evade capture would have been shattered after his arrest.

Crown prosecutor Knight poked holes in Dr Listwan's theories, showing that he hadn't even bothered to note the chronological order of Scanlon's crimes.

Q: You do not know whether the time when he went into the room carrying a billet of wood and striking the girl on the head was one of the first or one of the last?

A: I think it was the first offence, the first offence where he caused grievous bodily harm.

Q: In fact it was six months after the first; it was not the first at all. I think you put that down in your report to the fact that he was nervous in his early stages.

A: No, I put it down to the fact he did not intend to cause grievous bodily harm and was in a panic.

Q: When a person takes a lump of hardwood into a room before anything has happened, and he did not have go there in any event, and he hits a sleeping girl on the head, do you think there is anything different about that from waking her up and then in a struggle hitting her on the head?

A: Yes, well it would be the same.

That Dr Listwan hadn't shown an interest in the order in which Scanlon had committed his crimes didn't help his credibility. Nor did a later line of questioning where his unfamiliarity with the case was highlighted.

Q: If he were not able to resist, when he went in there and saw a sleeping woman and he had a knife or a razor blade in his hands, he would cut them on the breasts, is that what you say?

A: Yes.

Q: The sergeant said there were a lot of [cases of trespass], that a lot of those occurred. But how many of those did you think to look up, in which he was with a sleeping woman and did not do anything in the nature of cutting breasts?

A: The reason –

Q: No. Did you bother to check and find out?

A: I think I traced the amount of cases. I followed the newspapers. It is difficult to say today but in my recollection there were a great number of cases of injuring the breasts or attempting to injure the breasts.

Q: Now, in how many cases did he not injure the breasts, the ones where there was no compulsion?

A: I could not give you the figure.

In trying to explain how Scanlon, whom he said was acting under irresistible compulsion to cut a woman, was able to resist that compulsion Dr Listwan offered the weak explanation that "at times conscious processes and willpower take charge in the last moment and stop a person from fulfilling a compulsive act". Elsewhere, he was unable to explain why Scanlon escalated things sometimes; hitting Meyer with a block of wood, punching Coleman in the face and knocking her unconscious.

The prosecutor also asked Dr Listwan if he was serious about the idea that Scanlon was driven by the need to be chased, even in the instance when he attacked the bedridden 72-year-old Mona Sumner. "Yes, generally he had this desire," the doctor replied. "I am convinced about it. In this particular case it is very difficult to give a psychological explanation for each particular case but I think personally he was aware there were other people in the house and that he created a stir-up, or wanted to create it, because of the other inhabitants."

Prosecutor Knight also asked if Dr Listwan was aware how many times Scanlon had been chased, who responded "many times". When it was pointed out that, in the 18 crimes he pled guilty, only one person ever chased him (Valerie Thompson's husband Ron), the doctor claimed it wasn't about *actually* being chased. "I am referring to the feeling of being chased, the feeling of running away. Actually he knew all the police cars were converging on him. He knew all the radios were alerted, so it was not absolutely necessary that he was bodily chased."

Soon after that, Dr Listwan would leave the stand with serious doubt cast over both his knowledge of the case and of his belief Scanlon was driven by compulsion – but only sometimes.

Dr Listwan had referred Scanlon to clinical psychologist Henry Fleming for an examination, who took the stand next. Like Dr Listwan, Fleming spoke in psychiatric jargon, which the prosecutor made fun of when it was suggested the test results showed Scanlon was about to start hearing voices. He questioned how anyone could determine whether someone was *soon* to start hearing voices. Mr Fleming couldn't give him a simple answer, eventually concluding "I feel I am not able to give you satisfaction here".

The prosecutor brought along his own psychiatrist, Dr John McGeorge, who had previously offered up opinions in the newspapers about the Kingsgrove Slasher. Most of which turned out to be wrong, such as his contention that the offender would have a hatred of women and would not get along well with others. With an actual person to study, Dr McGeorge redeemed himself somewhat – and managed to keep the jargon to a minimum. He said

Scanlon possessed sadistic tendencies and while he could control them, chose instead to give into them, moving from being a peeping Tom, to breaking into houses and then assaulting women.

Dr McGeorge said Scanlon genuinely believed his motivation for committing his crimes was the thrill of the chase. "I think he honestly believed that to be so; although I do not think it is so," Dr McGeorge said. "He will not admit to himself that the basis of it all is simply the infliction of pain from which he must derive certain satisfaction."

Scanlon had derived so much enjoyment from this that Dr McGeorge felt it would be very difficult for him to overcome his urges. "It is possible to go from the simple infliction of linear cuts with a razor blade to mutilation of the victim," he said.

In cross examination, Dr McGeorge confirmed he thought Scanlon sane but "was quite prepared to concede he is abnormal". He also agreed with earlier testimony that he was in need of psychiatric treatment.

After the doctor left the stand, Justice Macfarlan adjourned the trial until Friday when Scanlon's barrister would get his last chance to sway the judge before the sentence was handed down.

38

"I don't want any mention of this hotel."
The owner of the Lavender Bay private hotel Scanlon stayed in just
after getting married, *Daily Mirror*, September 13, 1959

When Isaacs started with his closing remarks it seemed as though he'd forgotten he was supposed to be on Scanlon's side. He referred to his client as living a "Jekyll and Hyde existence"; he was a "decent sort of citizen" when the sun was up, but when night fell he committed "strangely bizarre and sadistic acts".

"What sort of an individual is this person," Isaacs asked, "who takes such glee in not merely the doing of the act, but in leaving his imprimatur, enjoying the knowledge of the notoriety that has been created and the hunt that ensues?

"Even in the absence of any medical evidence one would not require any great exercise of intuitive thinking to conclude that this man is 'not all there' – that there is some kink somewhere."

He went on to classify his client as sane but also a "sex-perverted psycho-neurotic" who suffered a "mental disease" that caused him to commit his crimes. But then he revealed the point of painting his client in such dark colours.

"If your Honour were dealing with an ordinary sort of individual I feel there would be very little I could say to induce your Honour to depart from imposing the maximum penalty," Isaacs said.

"However, you are dealing with an extremely abnormal individual … and the greater the degree of abnormality which you are prepared to attribute to such a person the further you will get away from maximum penalties."

In other words, my client is abnormal so he deserves a reduction in his sentence. Isaacs also suggested Scanlon's treatment would take between one to two years and, if that was not successful, then some sort of brain operation might be required (which the *Mirror* leapt on for their front page "Slasher may have surgery on brain").

Scanlon should get that treatment in prison, Isaacs said, and if it worked he should be allowed to spend the major part of his sentence on a prison farm. But that sentence shouldn't be too long, for Scanlon's sake.

"I would urge your Honour to give him hope of being able, at some time in the future, to be a completely rehabilitated citizen," Isaacs said. "Also to give him hope that he may look forward to the day when he will have expiated his crime, paid his debt to society and be once more permitted to join the free world."

Justice Macfarlan decided to delay his ruling on sentencing for a week, which gave the *Mirror* reporters the time to chase up some of his victims and ask if they still had some hard feelings. Ex-soldier Reg Geyson, father of victim Gloria, admitted he stayed up at night for months afterwards armed with – curiously – two pieces of Indian cane, just waiting for the Slasher to come back. "I would have killed him – army style, Reg said. "One piece of cane was to hold him off and the other was to hit him. But I don't feel bitter about him now."

Reg said his wife and daughter felt sorry for him; when the former saw Scanlon in court she thought "he looked like a nice fellow".

Rosalie Meyer, who Scanlon attacked with a piece of wood in November 1956, said she was over it all. "I don't care what happens now. It was a long time ago. Everything is back to normal. I am not bitter." For 72-year-old Mona Sumner, there was no use in worrying about it seven months after the attack. "If he is sick, he needs help. I was angry on the night but I am not now. These sort of things happen."

Scanlon's other senior citizen victim Marguerite Austin was not as willing to let bygones be bygones. "I don't forgive him and I don't feel sorry for him," she told the *Mirror*. "They ought to shoot him."

Capital punishment wasn't an option for Justice Macfarlan; instead he could only hand out jail time to Scanlon. And on Friday, September 18 – with around 20 people in the public gallery – he would deliver that sentence as Scanlon stood in the dock with his hands behind his back. It didn't take him long – his comments and the sentence took the Justice just two minutes.

"Your counsel has said, and I agree with him, that if nothing more appeared, the nature of your crimes merits the infliction of the maximum penalty," Macfarlan said.

"He has, however, persuaded me that weight must be given in regard to your previous blameless life, your previous good character and to the esteem in which you are still held by people who know you.

"However, you knew what you were doing and you knew what you were doing was wrong.

"I have given the greatest consideration to every aspect of your case."

Then he hung a long sentence around Scanlon's neck – 104 years for the 18 charges. However, the Justice said two of the sentences would be served consecutively – 10 years for the vicious July 1956 assault on Lesley Coleman and eight years for cutting Valerie Thompson in October of the same year. The sentences for the remaining 16 offences – including 10 years for the assault on Rosalie Meyer and eight years each for the Gaffey, Batger, Austin, Palmer and Sumner attacks – would be served concurrently.

When Scanlon was led from the dock to the cells soon afterwards, he started laughing and joking with the other prisoners. He would tell one of them that he found his sentence "a bit hot". The *Daily Mirror* would quote an unnamed leading criminal lawyer, who said Scanlon's sentence was longer than the 10-year average served by those convicted of manslaughter – apparently overlooking the fact Scanlon had committed 18 separate crimes and not just one. There was at least one anomaly in the sentencing; the break and enter of the Nicholls' home, where nothing but a bedsheet was cut, drew the same three-year sentence as the slashing attack on Margaret Campbell while she sat in a car.

On the day of Scanlon's sentencing *The Mirror* ran an interview with his wife Jean, where she said she had been visiting him at Long Bay. "We never talk about the case and we never talk about the future," she said. "We just talk about ourselves." However, some of the quotes attributed to Jean don't quite ring true; they sound as though they've been massaged – or perhaps even made up. "I'm so bewildered and so upset, I just can't believe it. It seems like some horrible nightmare that eventually I must awaken from. We were so happy in our love. We did everything together. We went to work together every morning. I just don't know what I'm going to do."

Night Terrors

By this time, her husband had been behind bars for almost five months – she had been there to visit him – and he'd gone through a committal hearing and pled guilty. But her remarks in this front-page story make it seem like she was only told days earlier what her husband had been up to and was still processing the information.

The verdict freed up the tabloid newspapers to run overviews of the case without the risk of being in contempt of court. On the day of the sentencing, the *Mirror*'s crime reporter Bill Jenkings wrote a piece headlined "The double life of the Slasher", in which he gave the background story on "the most amazing case in Sydney CIB history".

In the piece he recreated the scene in the Scanlons' Arncliffe flat on the morning of May 1, when Doyle brought David home to tell Jean what had been happening. "Anguished sobs showed how grievously Scanlon's confession had hurt the woman he loved," Jenkings' overly dramatic story read.

He also detailed the various groups within the Slasher Patrol; the lovers (with one male officer in drag), the racers (officers in "souped up vehicles") and the commandos (men hiding in the swamps wearing camouflaged clothing). "Being assigned to this patrol had been likened to being sent to Siberia," he wrote.

Two days later *The Mirror* followed it up with another piece tagged "The Slasher's private life", which was far less salacious than the headline suggested, The subhead – "budgies … and sweet peas" – was more honest as the piece covered some of the ordinary, mundane details of Scanlon's home life. Reporter Frank O'Neill had gone down to the Scanlons' Arncliffe home and peered over the fence, seeing the sweet peas blooming and the budgies Scanlon kept as pets.

"I cried," remembered his landlady when she heard he had been arrested. "I think every woman in this street cried. I just couldn't believe it ... not Dave."

The *Telegraph* also wrote of the efforts to catch the Slasher. "For three years, the Slasher evaded one of the most intense police hunts ever organised," the story read. It also contained information no other paper had reported; an organised effort from police to collect every adult male's fingerprints in the Slasher's territory, after he started his second series of attacks.

"They began a house-to-house canvass in the Slasher area, asking every male between the age of 15 and 45 to submit to a fingerprint test.

"Few refused, because everyone in the area had become intensely aware of the danger of a visit from the Slasher. Thousands more men were stopped at night in the streets in the area and fingerprinted."

The collection of as many as 100,000 fingerprints failed to identify Scanlon because it "stopped just two streets short of the Slasher's front door," the *Telegraph* claimed.

Perhaps the biggest scoop came from *Mirror* reporter Nancy Thom, who realised she'd met Scanlon before – she had stayed in the same Lavender Bay hotel as the newlyweds.

"There were 70 other guests," Thom wrote. "But not one of us thought for one moment that the David Scanlon we knew could possibly be the notorious person so vigorously pursued by the police."

She and the other guests would see Scanlon leave to "train" for athletics at night – not putting together the fact he was wearing the same clothes as the Slasher. "The evidence was right in front of our eyes continually, yet not one of us had even the haziest thought of connecting this young athlete with the man hunted by scores of policemen."

A large part of the reason she said he escaped everyone's attention was that he seemed so nice, not at all like the heinous villain who would commit crimes like the Slasher's.

"David Scanlon was one of the most personable, attractive young men I have ever met," she wrote. "He had charm, a good speaking voice and was always most courteous – particularly to elderly women guests residing in the house."

He and Jean didn't really mix with the other guests, she wrote, only requiring each other's company. "To the outsider, they were a young couple completely wrapped up in each other."

That was now no longer the case.

39

"Scanlon will definitely not be appealing."
Solicitor Bruce Miles, *Telegraph*, September 24, 1959

On the night of April 30, 1959, Freda Grafton had been at home in her bedroom. She was shocked to see a man's hand reaching in through her window. Hearing her scream, her husband called the police, who quickly arrived on the scene.

That was the night Scanlon was caught, and Grafton felt that the phone call her husband made meant they should get part – if not all – of the £1000 reward the government had put up to help capture the Slasher. In July the police commissioner disagreed, rightly claiming her information didn't contribute to Scanlon's arrest.

Her local MP and deputy Liberal leader Eric Willis took her cause to state parliament in November, claiming her "prompt action" led to Scanlon's capture. "In view of the obvious relationship between Mrs Grafton's telephone call to the police department," he said on the floor of parliament, "and the arrest a short time later of this criminal I would be obliged if you would reconsider this attitude in the hope that something can be done for Mrs Grafton."

He asked Premier Bob Heffron, who was also the police minister, to conduct a review of the decision not to pay the reward to Grafton. Willis would get no joy and Grafton would get no money. Heffron ordered the review which came back with the same result – "… after fully reviewing the matter [the acting deputy police commissioner] is satisfied that the decision not to pay the reward or any part of it to Mr or Mrs Grafton is fully justified."

Despite thinking his 18-year jail term was "a bit hot", Scanlon initially had every intention of serving out the sentence. His barrister Kingston told *The Sun* that he had spoken to his client in Long Bay about an appeal just a few days after his sentencing, suggesting there was a good chance it would be successful in reducing his time in jail. "But he has made up his mind definitely that he will not appeal," Kingston said.

A few months in a cell at Long Bay must have changed Scanlon's feelings on spending a total of 18 years behind bars. On February 17, 1960, an application on his behalf was lodged with the Court of Criminal Appeals. "The grounds for the appeal," *The Sun* reported, "is that the sentence imposed by Justice Macfarlan in September last year was too severe." The report also noted the earliest Scanlon could be released was 1971, depending on his behaviour.

The appeal made its way into court on March 25, where his barrister Simon Isaacs said Scanlon's sentence should be reduced to no more than 10 years. Scanlon himself was not in court for the appeal, held before three justices, including Chief Justice and former federal Labor minister Herb "Doc" Evatt.

Isaacs said the 18-year sentence would "smash and destroy" any hope of self-rehabilitation and that a 10-year sentence would serve as both a sufficient punishment and deterrent. Seeking to diminish the nature of the crimes, Isaacs said Scanlon had not sexually interfered with any victims and only used violence twice. The barrister also suggested the sentencing was motivated by a need to satisfy the press and the public. "I submit that protection of the public should not be associated with imposing a sentence that might be popular with the public or create outbursts in the press," he told the appeals court.

Justice Herron felt perhaps his fellow Justice Macfarlan thought Scanlon "had shown over a long period of time that he was unfit to live in close contact with ordinary society." He added that criminals seemed to think some sort of "discount" should be forthcoming after committing a number of crimes. He gave this example; if the penalty for car theft was three years, a man stealing a car on three successive nights should be sentenced to nine years.

"In this case your client committed offences in 1956 and again in 1958 and 1959," Justice Herron said to Isaacs. "Why should this not be given separate consideration?"

Justice Brereton added that Scanlon's offences could not be seen as "a single escapade".

"Medical evidence suggests," Isaacs replied, "that it was all part of the one mental aberration."

The three justices would defer their decision until March 29, where they rejected Scanlon's appeal. Chief Justice Evatt's ruling stated Justice Macfarlan acted out of sense of "duty" in sentencing Scanlon to 18 years.

"The pain, suffering, injuries and gross indignities inflicted upon women and children in the commission of these 18 separate crimes were disgraceful and degrading," Chief Justice Evatt said.

"The offences involved deliberate cunning and the long-sustained invasion of the privacy of the home. There was widespread fear and apprehension amongst the community.

"The nervous shock inflicted on so many innocent people was very great indeed. The recurrence of crimes of this type must be prevented by the organised community with the full vigour and justice of the law.

"It is impossible to shrink from the conclusions reached by Justice Macfarlan as to the sentences imposed. He paid proper regard to the possibility of psychiatric attention to, and treatment of, the applicant.

"In fixing the sentences Mr Justice Macfarlan had to face an extraordinary and responsible task. In my view he carried it out with compassion and yet with courage and a deep sense of duty to the public as well as to those who suffered from his dreadful crimes.

"In my opinion, the sentences were rightly imposed and the application should be dismissed."

The other two justice agreed. Scanlon, who had stayed in his cell at Long Bay rather than being brought to hear the decision, would not be leaving jail for at least the next 10 years.

40

"[Police] denied that Kingsgrove residents were being terrorised at night as during the attacks of the Kingsgrove Slasher."
Sydney Morning Herald, November 11, 1962

N ot long after his appeal failed, Scanlon was moved from Long Bay to Goulburn jail. While in a cell there, Scanlon would receive some bad news on May 23, 1961 – his wife Jean had started divorce proceedings. By this time Jean had moved to Berner Street in the southern Newcastle suburb of Merewether and was working as a shop assistant. She wanted the divorce on the grounds of desertion. According to the court papers, Jean was led to consider the marriage "terminated" on April 30, 1959, the date of his arrest.

"The respondent deserted the petitioner for two years and upwards from the time of his arrest by the NSW Police on the 30th April, 1959, and his removal from the matrimonial home, inasmuch as the separation so caused was the natural and probable result of his earlier premeditated and wrongful conduct and, therefore, a knowledge of, and intention to bring about, that result must be imputed to him," the petition read.

Scanlon opted not to contest the matter and the divorce was finalised on September 28, 1961, just a day shy of what would have been their fifth wedding anniversary.

While in prison, Scanlon worked in the bakery and did his time quietly. Though he did draw attention to himself during foot races held by the prisoners. In her book *The Taint*, Cheryl Jorgensen interviewed prisoner Ray Ide, who was in Goulburn prison at the same time as Scanlon. "Dave never got ruffled and I never heard him use a rude word or say anything bad about anybody," Ide said. "He was quietly doing his time, working in the baker's shop, speaking politely to everyone."

The big foot race was the mile – four laps of the jail's perimeter fence. Closely watched by the prison guards on the wall, of course. Ide remembered that Scanlon would win the mile race by a wide margin – he was clocking under five minutes. So Ide decided to try and beat him; he would train outside every day and run up and down the cells at night.

On the day of the race, Ide shot out of the blocks and ended up three-quarters of a lap in front, then let them catch up, before speeding off on the last lap – and he beat Scanlon. "I enjoyed that," he said. "I enjoyed beating the bloke they called the Kingsgrove Slasher."

As Scanlon served his time in prison, the career of the man who captured him moved ahead in leaps and bounds. For his work on the Kingsgrove Slasher case, Doyle had been awarded the Peter Mitchell Trophy for outstanding police work. The case had also boosted his profile. In 1960 he would play a crucial part in investigating the kidnapping and murder of eight-year-old Graeme Thorne, whose father Basil had just won £100,000 (equivalent to almost $3 million in 2018) in the lottery. Investigations centred on Stephen Bradley, who had fled the country by ship. Doyle was one of the officers who met the ship at Ceylon (now Sri Lanka) to arrest him.

On the flight home, Bradley would write and sign a confession – which he later retracted. It was to no avail; he would be found guilty and sentenced to life in prison. He was at Goulburn jail the same time as Scanlon, but would die of a heart attack in 1968.

Doyle would also regularly make the papers throughout the 1960s, for cases including a siege where a man had holed up in a house – Doyle crossed the road in full view of the gunman to drive away the car containing the body of the gunman's mother-in-law in case she was still alive and he could help. Doyle also worked on the theft of a yacht from Lord Howe Island that ended up almost 900 kilometres away at Norfolk Island.

The detective sergeant also played a part in the tragic tale of seven-month-old Glenda James. On September 16, 1965, her mother Sandra called police and said her baby Glenda had been taken from her pram after she left it outside a Merrylands supermarket.

"I could see the pram from inside the supermarket and checked it at least three times," she told the *Sydney Morning Herald*. "When I came out about a half-hour later the pram was still in its place but Glenda was missing." Police scoured the area, searching parks, playground and vacant land but could find no sign of Glenda.

A worker at the supermarket said they saw a blonde woman near the pram, who was driving a very similar car to one a watchman reported seeing rushing out of the car park. The search would drag on through the weekend, as Sandra made a fresh plea for the person to return her daughter safely; "I know my baby must still be alive. No one could kill my little baby."

Police followed every angle; they even chased up a report of a woman who returned home to her Bondi flat with a new baby (it was her own; the informant who lived in the same block of flats as the woman had failed to notice she was pregnant). By the end of September Premier Robert Askin announced a £1000 reward for the safe return of Glenda. A week later, Glenda's body was found in a vacant lot – by a man who claimed to have been led there because of a dream he had.

The case would soon take a dramatic twist nine hours after the discovery when the police charged Sandra with falsely reporting Glenda had been abducted. Instead, they believed Glenda had died of natural causes and Sandra had hidden her body in the vacant block less than a kilometre from her home.

In court police would allege Sandra found her child, who had been sick and was not feeding well, dead in the stroller at home and then left her body in the lot on the way to the supermarket. Detective Inspector Moye claimed Sandra told him Glenda had died at home overnight. "I don't know what made me think of doing it. I thought everyone would blame me and Frank [her husband] would not feel the same."

But Sandra would continue to insist in court that Glenda was taken from outside the supermarket. Oddly, her husband Frank, who lived at home with his wife and children, would testify that the last time he saw his daughter was four days before she was reported missing. Sandra would be committed to trial, where she decided to plead guilty and received a $100 good behaviour bond.

Scanlon would have to wait more than 10 years before he could walk the streets again. On March 26, 1970, he would pass through the prison gates on parole. He would have to report to a probation officer for the next seven years, after which his 18-year sentence would be complete.

Despite that passage of time, the public hadn't forgotten about him. Both *The Mirror* and *The Sun* would report on his release; the latter stating he was believed to be living with relatives in Sydney's eastern suburbs. In April, less than a month after his release, he would turn up at the offices of *The Telegraph* to talk to journalist Bryan Boswell – accompanied by two probation officers. Scanlon arrived in a grey sports coat, pressed trousers and shoes "shining like twin mirrors". Like many others, Boswell found Scanlon quiet, well-spoken and courteous. So quiet, in fact, that he didn't want to talk about anything he'd done. "I'm not going to say anything about what happened, or about my life in prison to anyone," he said. "It's in the past and that's that. I may want to get married again and have children. It's best my background is forgotten."

In a less-than-illuminating interview, he mentioned he had an unnamed day job in the city (a curfew limited his ability to ply the baking trade he learned in jail) and that, in a few walks around town he noticed things had changed. And then he largely disappeared from the public eye.

In 1979, after Brian Doyle's sudden resignation from the position of Senior Assistant Commissioner of Police, *The Mirror* would run a series of stories about the cases he worked on. The Slasher case warranted a full page to itself, in which Doyle suggested he had kept in touch with Scanlon. "David is doing very successfully since his release from prison and I would hate to see him embarrassed," the retired policeman said. "In fact he is a terribly nice fellow. He and I got along famously right from the start. I could only describe him as being a terribly good bloke."

Relatives of Scanlon suggest he spent some time in Morrisset psychiatric hospital on the NSW Central Coast, where he met a nurse. The 1977 and 1980 NSW electoral rolls list a David Joseph Scanlon living in Toronto, just 20 kilometres from the hospital, with a woman named Colleen. If a gravestone at Richmond is any indication, they may have had children. The marker bears both his full name and his correct birthday of October 4, 1929 and the inscription "Beloved husband, father and grandfather – sadly missed". The date of his death was July 14, 1995 – he was 65 when he died, having been a free man for 25 years.

And gradually, the story of what he did over those years in the late 1950s, would begin to fade too.

AFTERWORD

*"After he went to prison his wife divorced him. Now, he understands, she
has remarried and she and her new husband have adopted a child."*
Sunday Telegraph, April 12, 1970

Wh
at you've just read is the factual account of the case of
the Kingsgrove Slasher. I've deliberately left out my own
views and theories up to this point so as not to confuse
what *actually* happened with what I think may have happened. That's
why I decided to contain my own observations to this section at the
end of the book.

The main thing to point out relates to Scanlon's reasons for
terrorising women in the suburbs for several years. He was insistent
that it was all about the chase; that the reason why he carried razor
blades and cut women was just a means to an end. He needed to do
something to get people to chase him and, so he decided that would
do the job. That is obviously a lie; though I'm not sure whether or
not Scanlon himself knew it. Maybe he understood the real engine
that was powering his actions but figured to tell the police would
result in a harsher jail sentence. Maybe he convinced himself it was
the thrill of the chase so as to protect himself from his own truth.

In all these attacks, there's seldom any sign of a chase. Ron
Thompson was the only resident who actually chased him and there
were only one or two instances of the police being on his tail. In

many of his raids, Scanlon's actions actually seemed designed to *avoid* a chase rather than instigate one. He never attacked an adult male, the person in the house most likely to jump out of bed and give chase. Also, in a number of attacks, he leapt out of the bedroom window as soon as the victim awoke and raised the alarm. That meant he was already gone before the other residents in the house arrived in the room. If your desire is to have someone chase you, wouldn't you at least wait in the room for others to arrive, so they could see you before you made your escape? Darting out as quickly as possible is a sign of someone who wants to get away, not someone waiting to be chased.

That's because it wasn't about the thrill of the chase. At least not entirely. While he probably did enjoy evading the police and the sense of superiority and cleverness that came with it, it didn't drive him to commit those 18 crimes. It seems clear to me his work with the razor was the main focus.

By Scanlon's own admission, he would prowl the streets for hours before the razor would come out. That prowling included going inside other people's houses and creeping around but not cutting anyone. But here's the thing – if it really was about nothing more than the chase, why didn't he disturb the residents in those houses and get them to chase him? Perhaps the earlier break-ins were part of the ritual, maybe they heightened the sexual tension so that the release was greater when he did cut some unsuspecting woman. We'll likely never know but it seems clear the break-ins committed before his slashings served some purpose he was reluctant to go without.

There is an obvious pattern of escalation in what Scanlon did. He started out as a peeping Tom, trawling the neighbourhood backyards and watching people through their windows. Over time, that likely no longer brought the same thrill, so he graduated to watching people from *inside* their own homes. He stood at the end of their beds and watched as they slept peacefully, sat on the lounge in the corner and watched in the darkness.

Soon it wasn't enough that he was in their houses; he wanted them to *know* he'd been inside their houses. So he slashed people while they were sleeping; and in this action it's impossible not to notice the clear sexual impulse. Those he slashed were overwhelmingly female. In the case of the attack on Lesley Coleman, there were signs he had also slashed the bed of a sleeping boy in the same house, but that was really the only time he used his razor on a male.

Of his 18 attacks, 17 involved attacks on people (in Noel Nicholls' house he slashed an empty bed). And all of those 17 attacks focused on a woman. Even when there was a man sleeping next to her – as Ron Thompson was when Scanlon cut his wife Valerie – he always went for the woman. The attacks show a clear obsession with breasts; a number of women were cut in that area, and he would also slice the buttons off their pajama jacket as if to expose them. The last few attacks before his capture showed a further escalation in that regard; he'd started violently groping the breasts of his teenaged victims. He grabbed them so hard that he left bruises in the shapes of his fingers. There's simply no way to see that as anything other than a sexually-driven urge.

However, in terms of escalation, the pattern of violence in Scanlon's attacks seems odd. Serial criminals tend to get more violent as they go along, but Scanlon's most physically gruesome attacks – punching Lesley Coleman and hitting Rosalie Meyer with a piece of wood – happened very early on in his three-year run (while Marguerite Austin – his 13th victim – suffered a deep abdominal wound I accept that Scanlon did not intend to do that). In terms of physical violence, he actually seems to be getting better, not worse.

But I think a different picture emerges when the sexual driving factor of Scanlon's crimes are considered. From that viewpoint, there is a clear pattern of escalation; from cutting away pajama buttons to expose breasts, nicking them with his razor to the vicious groping of his last few victims. The physical violence of his early crimes may well be an outward manifestation of his efforts to tamp down his sexual drives; a violence that disappears once he gave into those other urges.

That then leads to the likely conclusion that his attacks would have gotten more sexually violent had he not been caught. The sexual aspect of some of his last attacks – those on Batger and Gaffey – are clear and was also a marked change from earlier assaults. Were he not caught, the treatment meted out to subsequent women and teens would have been far worse as Scanlon raised the stakes chasing the same sexual thrill.

Some sources post-2000 have given Scanlon's last name as "Scammony", leading to the assumption that he had been given a new identity by the government. To me, that is clearly an incorrect assumption; I cannot see the government creating a new identity for a criminal. New identities are to protect witnesses giving evidence not criminals who gave been released from jail.

The source of the "Scammony" name seems to be journalist Malcolm Brown's 2002 obituary of Brian Doyle, which refers to the Kingsgrove Slasher as one "David Joseph Scammony". Efforts made to contact Brown to ask where he got the name were unsuccessful. The Scammony name also appears in several of those "today in history" pieces syndication companies supply to newspapers. As a journalist, I know those history pieces are cut and pasted from one year to the next, so a mistake with a name in one year will continue to appear in subsequent years until finally picked up and changed. The likelihood is high that the "Scammony" name was just a mistake that gained a life of its own.

There is one question that remains unanswered – did Scanlon go back to his old ways after his release from jail? Efforts I made to get access to his criminal and jail records under freedom of information were unsuccessful, so we don't know what sort of treatment he got in prison. Did he get that brain operation his lawyer spoke of in court? Was his desire to commit future crimes shattered by the realisation he was not a criminal mastermind, as the psychiatrist at his trial suggested?

A search through online newspaper archives does not offer up any post-1970 crimes that are similar to those of the Slasher's. And one would assume a close eye was kept on him during his years of parole after 1970. Maybe he had learned how to better control himself; after all, Scanlon did manage to take a break of more than a year during his spree in the late 1950s.

Or maybe there are long-unsolved crimes on the Central Coast, where he settled after his release, just waiting to be connected to David Scanlon.

ACKNOWLEDGEMENTS

Night Terrors simply would not exist without access to a lot of contemporary sources.

The backbone of this book is the newspaper coverage of the case. I spent plenty of time at the State Library of NSW trawling through microfilm copies of Sydney newspapers of the late 1950s. Also, Lyn MacCallum from the *Sydney Morning Herald* library granted me access to the *Herald*'s substantial clipping file on the Kingsgrove Slasher, which included cuttings from *The Herald*, *The Sun*, *The Mirror* and *The Telegraph*. Sarah Gregory at the State Archives was exceptionally helpful in tracking down the documents they had on file. This includes the Scanlons' divorce papers and the testimony from David Scanlon's trial. She also found the sealed transcripts from his committal hearings and advised me on how to get access to them.

Thanks also goes to the Supreme Court staff who decided to waive the 75-year seal on the 1959 committal transcripts so I could look through them. Peter Doyle's piece about his uncle Brian Doyle called 'Stranger in the House' was a handy source of information – and a great read.

His short documentary – *Slasher Patrol* – made by The Guardian Australia is well worth watching. You can find that on YouTube.

Noelene, a family researcher, was able to help me piece together a little about happened to David Scanlon after his release from prison. And my dad willingly put up with my pestering about what he remembered of the Kingsgrove Slasher, having grown up in the suburb at the time.

Glen Humphries

BIBLIOGRAPHY

BOOKS and DOCUMENTS

Blainey, Geoffrey, *The Story of Australia's People: The Rise and Rise of a New Australia*, Penguin Random House, 2016

Cassidy, John, 'The Hell-raiser', *The New Yorker*, September 11, 2000

Doyle, Peter, 'Stranger in the House', *Sydney Review of Books*, November 14, 2016

Doyle, Peter, 'The Kibitzing Archive', *Text Journal*, Issue 18, October 2013

Duffy, Michael, and Hordern, Nick, *Sydney Noir: The Golden Years*, New South, 2017

Featherstone, Lisa, and Kaladelfos, Amanda, *Sex Crimes in the Fifties*, Melbourne University Press, 2016

Hickie, David, *The Prince and the Premier*, Angus & Robertson, 1985

Hill, Ron, and Madden. Brian, *Kingsgrove: the First Two Hundred Years*, Canterbury District and Historical Society, 1984

Jenkings, Bill, *Crime Reporter*, Horwitz, 1966

Jorgensen, Cheryl, *The Taint*, Boolarong Press, 2008

McDonald, Philippa, 'Nanny Goat Hill anniversary a modern-day reminder of people power', ABC News website, May 22, 2017

Moore, Nicole, *The Censor's Library*, University of Queensland Press, 2012

Murray, Therese, *1956: The Year that Rocked Kingsgrove*, self-published, 2014

Murray, Therese, *The Kingsgrove Slasher: St George's own Dr Jekyll and Mr Hyde 1956-59*, self-published, 2012

NSW Hansard, 'Kingsgrove Slasher' motion, December 9, 1958

NSW Hansard, 'Kingsgrove Slasher, December 10, 1958

NSW Hansard, 'Reward for Kingsgrove Slasher', November 24, 1959

NSW Hansard, 'Kogarah Police Station', November 25, 1959

NSW Hansard, 'Reward for Kingsgrove Slasher', December 2, 1959

NSW Hansard, 'Road Maintenance (Contribution) Amendment Bill', April 28, 1964

NSW Hansard, 'Crimes (Amendment) Bill', November 17, 1966

Police versus David Joseph Scanlon, Kogarah Local Court, June 1959

Regina vs David Joseph Scanlon, Central Criminal Court, September 1959

Scanlon vs Scanlon divorce papers, 1555/1961

Tedeschi, Mark, *Kidnapped: The Crime that Shocked a Nation*, Simon & Schuster, 2015

Tuchin, Greg, *My Father's Crimes*, Lulu, 2013

Whitton, Evan, *Can of Worms II*, Fairfax Library, 1986

Writer, Larry, *Razor*, Pan Macmillan, 2001

Glen Humphries

NEWSPAPERS

Canberra Times
'18 years gaol sentence for slasher', September 19, 1959
'Alleged slasher sent for trial', June 19, 1959
'Appeal to slasher's doctor', December 13, 1958
'Bomb explosion under car planned a month' August 15, 1956
'Decision held on appeal by slasher', March 26, 1960
'Gasometer explodes in Sydney', February 16, 1956
'Pleads guilty to slasher charges', September 8, 1959
'Police claim arrested man is slasher', May 2, 1959
'Police combing bushland for prowler', December 11, 1958
'Police say clerk admits to being slasher', June 17, 1959
'Slasher lived 'Jekyll and Hyde' life, court told', September 12, 1959
'Slasher out', April 1, 1970
'Slasher suspect released', December 12, 1958
'Suicide note confession to murder', September 25, 1956
'Women tell court of slashings', June 18, 1959

Canterbury-Bankstown Express (online)
'Canterbury's criminal history highlighted in new exhibition featuring the
Kingsgrove Slasher', Cindy Ngo, May 18, 2016

Central Queensland Herald
'Engineer leaves confession in car bomb case', August 16 1956

Daily Mirror/Sunday Mirror
'18 years for the slasher', September 18, 1959
'Appeal by Slasher', February 17, 1960
'Aust-wide hunt for clue to Slasher', February 15, 1959
'Bedroom slashing', December 20, 1956
'Caused her intense pain', June 16, 1959

Night Terrors

'Clothes hacked', February 13, 1959

'Did Slasher go abroad?', April 19, 1959

'Enjoyed thrill of chase', September 7, 1959

'Face to face with Slasher', December 10, 1958

'Fear fills their night', February 15, 1959

'Fluid gun to beat Slasher!', March 26, 1959

'Girl (14) terrorized in new Slasher outrage', February 13, 1959

'Girl, 16, scares intruder', January 28, 1959

'Girl became hysterical', June 17, 1959

'Girl feared Slasher', December 18, 1956

'Girl of ten as witness', June 18, 1959

'Girl scared to be alone', June 17, 1959

'Girl victim pestered police say', December 15, 1956

'Gunmen wait for Slasher', August 29, 1956

'Help trap the Slasher', February 13, 1959

'I left my trademark', June 16, 1959

'I'm the Slasher, love', October 16, 1979

'I'm your man – I'm the Slasher', June 16, 1959

'I never suspected', Nancy Thom, September 22, 1959

'I still can't believe it – wife', September 18, 1959

'I wanted to waken her', September 16, 1959

'Intruder startles girl (19), December 16, 1959

'Man at girl's curtains', December 8, 1958

'Man in mask caught', August 23, 1956

'Man on trespass charge', August 23, 1956

'Man tells girl 'I'm the Slasher'', December 17, 1958

'Maniac Slasher returns', November 19, 1958

'More police plea', December 10, 1958

'Night noise scare', August 1, 1956

'Picks house near scrub', February 11, 1959

'Police baffled by new attacks', December 4, 1958

'Police hunt razor fiend', October 29, 1956

'Police within 20 yds', March 12, 1959

'Pretty girl bashed', November 26, 1956

'Prowler escapes by leap', December 9, 1958

'Prowler scares woman', April 11, 1959

'Prowler slashes bedding in home', August 15, 1956

'Prowler spotted by nun', December 19, 1959

'Prowler's close shave again', February 25, 1959

'Prowlers terrify women', November 20, 1958

'Raid in a new suburb alarms police', December 22, 1958

'Remand without bail', May 1, 1959

'Residents in nightly fear', February 14, 1959

'Scare for girl', 31 July, 1956

'Schoolgirls tell – terrified by night intruder', June 18, 1959

'Sex slasher attacks girl in bedroom', June 28, 1956

'Sheahan calls to Slasher', March 13, 1959

'Shock 'bodily harm' claim', June 18, 1959

'Slash maniac hunt', February 12, 1959

'Slash probe: man quizzed', September 13, 1956

'Slasher: 18 years. Appeal denied', March 29, 1960

'Slashed victims tell of night raids', June 17, 1959

'Slasher attack at show', March 26, 1959

'Slasher caught say police', May 1, 1959

'Slasher deserves 18 years – victim', September 18, 1959

'Slasher footprint found in mud', March 18, 1959

'Slasher given 18-year goal term', September 18, 1959

'Slasher guilty!', September 7, 1959

'Slasher has escape ready,', February 11, 1959

'Slasher history – crime first of kind in the world', September 7, 1959

'Slasher in weird attack – maniac gashes girl (14)', December 14, 1956

'Slasher may have surgery on brain', September 11, 1959

'Slasher report a hoax', February 21, 1959

'Slasher sends letter to Mirror', December 24, 1958

'Slasher strikes again, escapes police net', December 11, 1958

'Slasher surgery hinted', September 11, 1959

Night Terrors

'Slasher tag unfair', May 2, 1959

'Slasher term 'too severe'', March 25, 1960

'Slasher territory', March 13, 1959

'Slasher's 17th victim', February 11, 1959

'Surprised near girl's bedroom', December 7, 1958

'Spun baby's cot around', June 17, 1959

'Sydney has 2nd slasher', February 16, 1959

'Terrified by prowler', February 18, 1959

'Terror in new slash attack', December 26, 1958

'Terror over Slasher', February 13, 1959

'Terrorised by Slasher', December 3, 1958

'The double life of the Slasher', Bill Jenkings, September 18, 1959

'The Slasher goes free', March 31, 1970

'The Slasher strikes again', December 11, 1958

'The Slasher's private life', Frank O'Neill, September 20, 1959

'Vigilantes out after prowler', August 21, 1956

'What has happened to the Kingsgrove Slasher', January 28, 1959

'Wife did not know', September 7, 1959

'Wife's nightwear hacked in terrifying attack in bedroom', December 11, 1958

'Women forgive the Slasher', September 13, 1959

'Yes, the Slasher struck again last night', February 13, 1959

'Women forgive the Slasher', September 13, 1959

Daily Telegraph/Sunday Telegraph

'25 razor slashes on girl's bed and clothes', August 19, 1956

'£500 to trap the Slasher offered', February 21, 1959

'18 charges cover three years', June 17, 1959

'Big police search for prowler', February 18, 1959

'Detective says man claimed to be Slasher', June 17, 1959

'Help trap the Slasher', February 13, 1959

'How Slasher was caught', September 20, 1959

'Intruder escapes in chase', February 25, 1959

'Man sent for trial: Police claim Slasher admission', June 19, 1959

'Man questioned after chase', May 1, 1959

'My wife was nervous of the Slasher', June 17, 1959

'Police race to trap Slasher', December 7, 1958

'Prowler flees in night', August 22, 1956

'Search for Slasher broadens', December 5, 1958

'Sex maniac's razor attack in bedroom', July 29, 1956

'Slasher: 18 years', September 18, 1959

'Slasher escapes cordon', December 10, 1958

'Slasher hunt hampered by hysteria', December 14, 1958

'Slasher in court, police say', May 2, 1959

'Slasher lived as master-mind in world of dreams', September 8, 1959

'Slasher thinks he's a surgeon', December 17, 1958

'Sleeping sisters attacked', February 24, 1959

'Supreme Court rejects appeal', March 30, 1960

'The Slasher escapes police traps', December 11, 1958

'The Slasher now just wants to forget it all', April 12, 1970

'Used slash as trade mark', September 8, 1959

'What manner of a man is the Kingsgrove Slasher?', February 20, 1959

'Woman in car says she found 12 cuts on body', June 18, 1959

'Women tell of attacks by night', June 18, 1959

'Youth held in mistake for Slasher', December 12, 1958

Melbourne Age

'18 years jail for the slasher', September 19, 1959

'100 police wait for slasher to strike', December 12, 1958

'Counsel's claim in slasher case', May 23, 1959

'Inter-state hunt for NSW slasher', February 16, 1959

'Kingsgrove Slasher loses appeal on sentence', March 30, 1960

'Slasher invited chase, court told', June 17, 1959

'Slasher on the prowl in Sydney again', December 23, 1958

'Sydney detectives appeal for slasher', December 5 1958

Night Terrors

Melbourne Argus
'Doctor, sister die in bomb outrage', August 14, 1956
'Experiment with death', August 15, 1956
'He thought for the living as he slew', September 25, 1956
'Screams foil attacker', July 30, 1956
'Sydney slasher attacks girl, 14', December 15, 1956
'Sydney slasher batters young girl', November 27, 1956
'The slasher's on the prowl again', December 20, 1956

Sydney Morning Herald/Sun Herald
'18-year gaol sentence for slasher', September 19, 1959
'20 degrees drop in city heat', December 21, 1956
'70mph pursuit of two in car', April 29, 1959
'Appeal on slasher renewed', March 13, 1959
'Armed robbery charges', November 12, 1958
'Armed wait for attack by slasher', December 9, 1956
'Bitter Cabinet spill over new police chief', November 25, 1976
'Bus into woman's bedroom', February 28, 1956
'Bottle slasher gaoled', July 13, 1956
'Cabinet appoints deputy to new police chief', December 16, 1976
'Call for launch', April 18, 1963
'CIB chief among promotions', April 16, 1957
'Clerk for trial; girls tell of night intruder', June 19, 1959
'Clue to slasher in prints', December 11, 1958
'Column Eight', December 10, 1958
'Conductor on bus theft charges', February 29, 1956
'Cornered man "snarls" at householder', December 8, 1956
'Day and night hunt for slasher', February 12, 1959
'Dingo attack to seduce young girl', October 3, 1958
'Doctor batters mother to death, suicides', January 28, 1956
'Doctor, sister killed in car bomb outrage in Kingsgrove', August 14, 1956
'False Banksia slasher scare', February 18, 1959

'Found guilty of manslaughter', April 15, 1955

'Freak storms in country', December 4, 1958

'Funeral of bomb victims, killer', August 16, 1956

'Gas blast called 'eruption'' February 16, 1956

'Girl's pyjamas cut', June 17, 1959

'Girls' school killer deranged, police say', August 5, 1955

'Head-on game with cars: youth gaoled', September 22, 1956

'Hottest day since 1954', December 20, 1956

'I need help! Mrs Bradley's plea from Aden', October 23, 1960

'Ice pick attack at phone box', February 5, 1957

'Intruder attacks sleeping girl, 14', February 24, 1959

'Intruder slashes clothing', December 20, 1956

'Judgment reserved in appeal for slasher for cut in sentence', March 26, 1960

'Jury acquits woman of murder charge', August 31, 1956

'Kingsgrove Slasher pleads guilty; master mind theory', September 8, 1959

'Kingsgrove Slasher set free', March 31, 1970

'Liked chase, police say', June 17, 1959

'Leave him to police', December 14, 1958

'Man's 12th attack on woman', November 27, 1956

'Man, 75, for trial on charge of attempted murder', May 18, 1956

'Man assaults widow, 85', November 11, 1962

'Man caught after chase', May 1, 1959

'Man confesses placing death car bomb', September 25, 1956

'Man fined: police bribe charge', September 26, 1958

'Man for trial', June 18, 1959

'Man slashes girl's face three times', February 16, 1959

'Man unfit to plead on murder charge', November 15, 1955

'Man who wanted to help the police', January 30, 1957

'Men in night hunt for gun prowler', May 4, 1956

'Men with knives', November 15, 1955

'Mental harm', March 1, 1959

Night Terrors

'Murder by floodlight', August 7, 1955

'Mother's bond', December 3, 1955

'Mother charged with murder', February 11, 1955

'Mother's 'nerves bad'', June 18, 1959

'Mother to face murder intent charge', September 27, 1955

'Mr Doyle just wants to set the record straight', October 8, 1979

'Nemesis of crims and corruption', Malcolm Brown, August 9, 2002

'New attack by Slasher', February 13, 1959

'New attack on sleeping woman', February 11, 1959

'New hope in blighted suburb', March 1, 1959

'New truck stolen and burnt', May 21, 1955

'No bond for bottle slasher', July 10, 1956

'Non-payment of reward: review urged', November 25, 1959

'Public responds to slasher appeal; new plans by police', February 14, 1959

'Police ask: do you know the slasher?', December 5, 1958

'Police force armed man to surrender', July 29, 1968

'Police in disguise', February 15, 1959

'Police name man in court as Kingsgrove Slasher', May 2, 1959

'Police on slasher hunt answer call', February 17, 1959

'Police solve major crimes', May 2, 1956

'Prowler gets away', December 9, 1958

'Public responds to Slasher appeal; new plans by police', February 14, 1959

'QC urges slasher be given chance to rehabilitate himself', September 12, 1959

'Questions on attack on girl', June 17, 1959

'Scalpel may be clue to Slasher', December 4, 1958

'Search for slasher: More than 120 police in manhunt', December 12, 1958

'Shark peril at beaches', March 8, 1956

'Skylarking with bus alleged: man is acquitted', February 6, 1957

'Slasher appeals against 18 years', February 17, 1960

'Slasher attacks sleeping woman', October 29, 1956

'Slasher fails in appeal', March 30, 1960

'Slasher hunt: girls now live in fear', August 19, 1956

'Slasher on North Shore', December 15, 1956

'Slasher scare at Ramsgate', December 16, 1958

'Slasher scare; man in chase', February 25, 1959

'Slasher scared off by girl's mother', December 11, 1958

'Slasher strikes again', February 11, 1959

'Slasher suspect released', December 12 1958

'Slasher will not appeal', September 24, 1959

'Slasher: woman hater says Dr', February 12, 1959

'Stepson on murder count', October 9, 1955

'Storm ends hottest day in three months', March 9, 1956

'Storms threat to city', February 14, 1959

'Story of bribe improbable, defence claims', October 21 1958

'Street prowler attacks women', October 5, 1956

'Suspected slasher seen twice more', December 10, 1958

'Tears as owners inspect damage to yacht', April 21, 1963

'The Slasher: His Mark', December 11, 1958

'The Slasher strikes again', August 15, 1956

'Thousands flock to beaches', November 26, 1956

'Threat to fair trial claimed', May 23, 1959

'Top policeman 'not deserting the ship'', Andrew Watson, October 7, 1979

'Two girls threatened with knife', October 21, 1958

'Two men steal £500 in hold-up', November 11, 1958

'Unrest in the police ranks', Peter Kennedy, October 11, 1979

'Victim saw bomb put on car, police believe', August 15, 1956

'Vigilantes patrol streets, search for the slasher', December 13, 1958

'Wide search for polite prowler after four attacks', May 11, 1959

'Witness says bomb threat against him', September 17, 1955

'Women tell court of night attacks and damaged clothes', June 18, 1959

'Weeping girl tells of attack by 'growling man'', June 17, 1959

Night Terrors

The Sun

'8 cars in in hunt', August 22, 1956

'A slashing night out', January 15, 1959

'Attacks on girls at night', December 4, 1958

'Arrest in swamp, May 1, 1959

'Attack story: Doctors tell of wounds', June 17, 1959

'Bizarre death of executive', March 28, 1957

'Call for £1000 reward', February 20, 1959

'Call from the Slasher?', December 10, 1958

'Calls flood police phone', December 5, 1958

'Dawn police chase', March 13, 1959

'Doctor's appeal to relatives', December 12, 1958

'Fathers to hunt Slasher', August 20, 1956

'Girl afraid to be alone', June 17, 1959

'Girl's bed ripped', August 15, 1956

'Girls tell court of attacks', June 17, 1959

'Girl fears dark', June 18, 1959

'Girls fear knife', December 4, 1958

'Kingsgrove Slasher set free', March 31, 1970

'Kogarah prowler chased', January 13, 1959

'Mad sex fiend out again', July 31, 1956

'Man eludes prowl patrol', February 23, 1959

'Man in mask caught', August 23, 1956

'Man on trespass charge', August 23, 1956

'Naked man's threat', November 20, 1958

'Near naked prowler', December 28, 1956

'No one's ever seen his face … the Kingsgrove Slasher', December 9, 1958

'Paint trap for Slasher', December 13, 1958

'Police probe slash story', December 20, 1956

'Prowler escapes: was it the Slasher', March 12, 1959

'Razor attach on girl', August 18, 1956

'Slashed! Fourth attack on a young mother', October 29, 1956

'Slasher: 18 years', September 18, 1959

'Slasher at work', December 3, 1958

'Slasher escapes', August 1, 1956

'Slasher gaoling a duty', March 29, 1960

'Slasher gets 18 years', September 18, 1959

'Slasher 'jitters' in suburb', February 16, 1959

'Slasher may be back', September 10, 1956

'Slasher method copied', February 25, 1959

'Slasher scare at window', December 18, 1959

'Slasher scared', December 27, 1956

'Slasher story: Girl hits out with shoe', June 18, 1959

'Slasher was here', December 21, 1956

'Slasher: Woman hater, says Dr', February 12, 1959

'Stalled, rapped, nabbed, freed', February 19, 1959

'Taxi man at CIB', January 7, 1959

'The day the Slasher was caught', September 7, 1959

'The Slasher asks 10 yrs or less', March 25, 1960

'The Slasher: Pleads guilty to 18 charges', September 7, 1959

'Trap for Slasher', February 13, 1959

'Told wife of working back', June 16, 1959

'Undies cut to pieces', December 19, 1956

'Urgent police appeal', March 12, 1959

'Youth's plucky pursuit', April 1, 1959

'Woman feared attack', April 11, 1959

United States newspapers

'Australian slasher sentenced', *Corpus-Christi Caller-Times*, September 18, 1959

'Kingsgrove Slasher' jailed for 18 years', *Poughkeepsie Journal*, September 18, 1959

'Man terrorising women for 4 years is caught', *Louisville Courier-Journal*, September 8, 1959

Night Terrors

'Slasher captured by Sydney police', *Arizona Republic*, September 8, 1959
'Slasher pleads guilty to counts in Sidney [sic] court', *Albuquerque Journal*,
September 9, 1959
'Slasher's reign of terror ends', *Philadelphia Inquirer*, September 19, 1959
'Terror slasher caught in Sydney', *Hartford Courant*, September 8, 1959

Woman's Day
'Fear comes to Slade Road', April 20, 1959

INDEX

If you liked this book why not check out my others, all which are available through my micropublishing company Last Day of School? (www.lastdayofschool.net)

The Slab
24 Stories of Beer in Australia

Beer. You know it and, chances are, you love it. But you might not know the part beer has played in Australian history. Right from the start beer was there. It was on board The Endeavour when Captain Cook set sail for Australia. It was drunk not long after the First Fleet landed in Botany Bay.

It was there when World War I soldiers got a skinful and ran riot in the streets of Sydney. It was there during the era of six o'clock closing where people were still drinking it long after the little hand had passed the six. It was even there when it really shouldn't have been - when Canberra declared itself an alcohol-free zone.

What? You didn't know the nation's capital used to be dry? Well, then you need this book. You'll also find out just what the hell Voltron has to do with Victoria Bitter.

"History as it should be written. With beer. About beer. Crisp. Refreshing. Won't cause bloat."
John Birmingham, author of Leviathan

"I thought I'd been asked to review Christos Tsiolkas' The Slap and was pleasantly surprised to find myself reading about beer. The Slab is a full-bodied book, with a fruity aftertaste and a nose that carries the slightest hint of sawdust and vomit. I suggest you XXXX it."
David Hunt, author of Girt

James Squire: The Biography

After getting caught swiping a few chickens from a neighbour, James Squire was sentenced to seven years in Sydney Cove. You could say it was the best thing he ever did – it led to him become a brewer, policeman, property tycoon, respected citizen and a bloody rich guy. All because of the theft of a few chooks.

But if all you know about James Squire is what you've read on labels on beer bottles, then you really don't know that much at all. This book – the first biography of Squire – separates the facts from the well-known myths about his life. He never stowed away on the First Fleet ship carrying female convicts, didn't get lashed for stealing the ingredients to make beer and might not have been the first person to grow hops in Australia.

He was also a man who may have used a false name on his daughter's birth certificate, loathed people who cut down trees on his property and got along far better with the natives than most of the other white newcomers.

Along the way you'll also discover a few other things about Sydney Cove, including Captain Arthur Phillip's efforts to get his hands on some Aboriginal heads for a friend, early Australians' fondness for cider rather than beer, the fight rival brewer John Boston had over a dead pig and the marine who tried to trade his hat for an Aboriginal child.

Friday Night at the Oxford

The story that led to reunion of legendary band Tumbleweed. An in-depth look at Sunday Painters, a band decades ahead of their time. Iconic shows like HOPE, HyFest and the Steel City Sound exhibition. These are just of the more than 100 stories about Wollongong bands and events written by journalist Glen Humphries for the *Illawarra Mercury*, from 1997 through to 2018, and his own short-lived website Dragster.

The 200-plus pages of *Friday Night at the Oxford* provide a snapshot of what happened in the Wollongong music scene over the last 20-odd years – the bands, the venues, the events. It's a celebration of the music of a city.

So dig it.

Sounds Like an Ending
Midnight Oil, 10-1 and Red Sails in the Sunset

In 1982, Midnight Oil was a band in trouble. Their last album, *Place Without a Postcard*, was supposed to be their big breakthrough but it hadn't worked out that way. So they found themselves in London, feeling the pressure of recording what was a "make or break" album. Members threatened to leave, others had nervous breakdowns and the ANZ bank manager back home was sweating as he watched the overdraft he'd approved for the band get bigger and bigger.

If this album went the same way as the last one, it could be the end of Midnight Oil. Out of the crisis came *10,9,8,7,6,5,4,3,2,1*, an album that changed everything for the band. It entered the charts and stayed there for more than three years. They started playing bigger venues - and they were able to pay back the bank manager.

Two years later, they headed to Japan to record the polarising *Red Sails in the Sunset*. It managed to do what *10-1* couldn't - give the band their first No1 album. But again the band found themselves facing the possibility it could all be over, courtesy of lead singer Peter Garrett's tilt at federal politics. If he wins, the band loses.

In *Sounds Like an Ending*, journalist and author Glen Humphries takes a track-by-track look at these two albums and the times and turmoil that fuelled them. That includes whether the *10-1* title was a sly dig at a certain Australian music TV show, the stories behind the songs and explaining what's really happening on the cover of *Red Sails in the Sunset*.

"I used to think that I was some kind of Oils authority. Then I read this book. Glen's the real expert. This is insightful and really entertaining."
Jeff Apter, author of *High Voltage*

EBOOKS
The Six-Pack
Stories from the World of Beer

From stories of monks making beer, to rumours of an unpleasant secret "ingredient" in a world-famous drink, there are plenty of great stories about beer. And six of them are captured in this ebook.

Beer is Fun!

Oh look, it's the best moments from Beer is Your Friend, the blog that won a national beer writing award and also inspired Dale to leave a comment "give ur self an uppercut u oxygen thief".

Clearly Dale wasn't on the judging panel. Which is a good thing too, otherwise I wouldn't have won that trophy – and who doesn't like winning trophies?

Why should you buy this book? Because it's 300-plus and it'll cost you just $2. What else in life will give you loads of entertainment for just $2? Go on, buy it. If you don't like it, I'll give you your money back. Well, that's a lie, I won't give you a cent, because I plan on holidaying in The Bahamas with the $2 you give me.